The POWER of a Transformed Wife

God's Design for Marriage:
How It Changed My Life
and Can Change Yours

by LORI ALEXANDER

© Copyright 2016 by Lori Alexander

ISBN 13: 978-0-9981687-0-8

eBook Editions:
Adobe Digital Edition 978-0-9981687-1-5 (.epub)
Kindle and MobiPocket Edition 978-0-9981687-2-2 (.prc)

All rights reserved. This book is protected by the copyright laws of the United States of America. This book may not be copied or reprinted for commercial gain or profit. No portion of this book may be reproduced, stored in a retrieval system, or transmitted in any form or by any means—electronic, mechanical, photocopy, recording, scanning, or other—except for brief quotations in critical reviews or articles, without the prior written permission of Lori Alexander.

Scripture quotations are taken from the King James Version. Copyright © 1982 by Thomas Nelson, Inc. Used by permission. All rights reserved.

Scripture quotations taken from the New American Standard Bible®
(NASB). Copyright © 1960, 1962, 1963, 1968, 1971, 1972, 1973, 1975, 1977, 1995 by the Lockman Foundation. Used by permission. www.Lockman.org.

Scripture quotations marked(NIV) taken from the Holy Bible, New International Version®, NIV ®. Copyright © 1973, 1978, 1984, 2010 by Biblica Inc. All rights reserved worldwide.

Published by Turning Page Books

Editorial assistance by Mike Yorkey (www.mikeyorkey.com), Sandy Reese, Kelley White, and Emily Alexander

Cover concept by Erin Alexander

Back cover photo by Lauren Natalie Photography (www.laurennatalie.com)

Cover and interior design by Blue Muse Studio (www.bluemusestudio.com)

For information on Lori Alexander, visit her blog at
www.lorialexander.blogspot.com.

To contact her, please email her at thetransformedwife7@gmail.com.

Dedication

To those women who dreamed of having a close and intimate marriage only to find out that their marriage was more like a nightmare.

Table of Contents

- A Note to the Reader 7
1. My Life Growing Up 13
2. Why I Mentor Women....................31
3. Let It Go!............................41
4. Allow Him to Lead 49
5. What Submission Looks Like............59
6. Easy Conflict Resolution 67
7. This Thing Called Sex 81
8. Winning Him Without a Word 91
9. Teaching and Training Children in the Way They Should Go 113
10. Birth Control and Having Children ...127
11. The Dating Scene and Sexual Purity ..133
12. Keepers at Home 149
13. How are You Dressing?................161
14. Talking About Your Financial Health .169
15. The Disciplined Mind: Trusting God and Doing Good 183
16. Clutter No More.....................195
17. Serving Healthy Foods Means Healthy Families ..205
18. A Way to a Man's Heart 223
19. The Power to Become a Transformed Wife 229
- About the Author.....................242

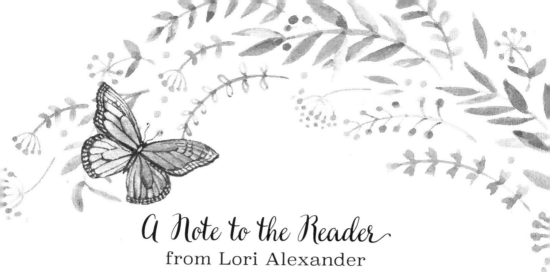

A Note to the Reader
from Lori Alexander

Are you in a difficult marriage or a marriage that's failing to meet your expectations of having a close and intimate relationship with your spouse?

Do you feel like you're taking one step forward only to have your hopes of a happy marriage dashed by a harsh word or one disappointment after another?

Does it seem like you're moving further away from your husband rather than toward him? And, lastly, is your unhappy marriage just another trial in life that you have to accept, or has God already given you the answers to all these struggles if you follow Him?

These questions became especially meaningful to me a few years ago when my husband, Ken, and I were walking around the park one day. As we were enjoying the fresh air and sunshine of San Diego, we wandered into a discussion of what would become of our marriage after the last of our four children flew from the nest. We were both concerned that the one common joy that seemed to hold our relationship together would soon be gone, and all that would be left would be the remnants of our disappointing marriage, held together only by our love for Jesus.

Ken shared what was on his heart with me. "I've been giving this some thought, and I've come to the conclusion that our marriage is just a partnership. I thought marriage was supposed to be about intimacy, closeness, and affection—not the distance, arguing, or upsets that have kept us from feeling closeness."

His words felt like a dagger plunged into my heart. What he said deeply saddened me, and I had no idea how to respond. The thought hit me that not only were we so different from each other, but there were few things we enjoyed doing together, apart from attending the children's sports and ballet events. After all, we argued about almost everything—even silly things—and we had been combative toward each other for a long time. In my mind, few things were off limits when it came to my desire to "fix" Ken and make him into the husband I thought he should be.

All of the conflict between Ken and me started on our honeymoon when I gave him a hard time for eating Ritz Crackers with fake cheese spread. This was in 1980—even before I knew anything about hydrogenated oils—and I was appalled that he would eat something so junky since I was raised to be a health nut.

In the ensuing years, there were times when I would give him the silent treatment for eating unhealthy foods. I would sit with a frown on my face, not saying a word, but he would get the point. I thought that if he really cared about my happiness, he wouldn't eat ice cream and deli meats. Unfortunately, food wasn't the only area shadowed by my disapproval. I also thought he watched too much television, was too consumed with sports, and was grumpy toward me.

Often, I acted more like his mother than his wife. I would be moody, upset, and often nag him in an attempt to influence him into doing what I thought was best. Looking back, I realize that a lot of my discontentment stemmed from feeling like Ken and I never connected in a meaningful way early on in our marriage. We may not have been able to verbalize it through all the turmoil, but I think we both realized that our relationship was not the way God intended it to be.

Thank goodness we had children. As each little one arrived, my life became increasingly immersed in our four kids. I didn't give much time to loving and caring for my husband, which meant I was a great mother but a neglectful wife. Ken and I weren't connecting at any deep level. Even when we went out for dates, we would frequently argue, spoiling the fun we were supposed to be having. There was no closeness or affection between us but just a continual undercurrent of conflict throughout our first twenty years of marriage.

After Ken uttered those piercing words at the park, I was heartbroken. He was verbalizing the truth about our disconnected marriage, which left me speechless. I felt grief as I finally came to realize that I had no idea how to fix our relationship.

I thought back to other times when we would take walks together and Ken would explain the things I was doing wrong. I hated when he did that because I thought he was trying to "fix" me.

What about him? Was he perfect? No.

He did things wrong also, and I had a long mental list of his faults to throw back at him in any discussion. But one thing we had agreed upon from the beginning was that divorce would never be in our vocabulary. Even if we had to "grin and bear it" and live with each other, we were going to be the vow keepers God called us to be.

After two decades of marriage, interspersed with some good times but far too many struggles, we still could not seem to reach a meaningful level of closeness and intimacy in our marriage. We were both solid believers who loved the Lord and knew the Word of God, yet we couldn't seem to find the oneness and harmony we knew God intended for us.

Then something remarkable happened that started me on my journey to becoming a "Transformed Wife." I came across a book entitled Created to Be His Help Meet by Debi Pearl, which woke me up to what I was missing in my marriage. Like the older, godly woman that she was, Debi mentored me through her book and taught me God's way of becoming the wife I was designed to be. Instead of doing marriage my own way and trying to control Ken, which only increased the feelings of separation between us, I began to search for ways that I could please my husband and follow God's plan for a strong marriage.

As I worked through my feelings, I realized that many years of tears and struggles could have been exchanged for fun and enjoyment. I could have had the intimate marriage I dreamed about growing up, where we shared our hopes and dreams together, instead of spending our time arguing and suffering in a distant marriage.

This is why I'm writing this book to help women who feel at a loss in their marriage. If this sounds like you—if you've tried counseling, reading books, and talking to other women, yet nothing seems to be working or making sense—I can help. Even if your marriage is falling apart, or you feel like giving up, or you find yourself headed for separation or divorce, it's not too late to save your marriage. God's Word teaches us in Titus 2 that the older women are to teach the younger women how to love their husbands, be pure, and run their households well. When you learn what I have learned on my journey to becoming a Transformed Wife, you will experience the peace that comes from giving up your own will and surrendering to God's plan.

You will find that once you relinquish the desire to be in control and rest in His perfect will, your marriage will be free to become the one you always dreamed of. Before we go much further, however, this would be a great time for me to tell you more about my journey—where my life began, what influenced me along the way, and how I eventually found the key to becoming a Transformed Wife.

1
My Life Growing Up

During the first twenty-three years of our marriage, I had all the excuses in the book as to why I was such a neglectful wife. The problem with every one of those excuses, however, is that none of them held me responsible for my part in all the drama. I was good at pointing fingers at Ken and laying the blame solely on him, but the truth is, most of our problems resulted from the deep-seeded rebellion in my heart. As you will soon discover, my story is one of pain and struggle. That's why when the women I mentor tell me about their problems, I usually just smile. I know what they're facing because I've been where they are.

I was raised in a Christian home in Canyon Country, California (thirty miles north of Los Angeles), with my younger sisters, Alisa and Debbi. My parents, Art and Ellen, loved Jesus and went to church faithfully, but they argued almost all the time when they were together. Part of it was because my mom grew up in a family with seven children while my dad was an only child, so they had different outlooks on life. Since they seldom agreed on anything, there wasn't much harmony in my home. As a hospital pathologist, my dad worked long hours, but when he was home, their "fireworks" of disagreement could be heard in the next room by their little girls waiting to fall asleep. Praise be to God, my parents have a fabulous marriage now after years of struggle. They are both eighty-five years old and love being married to each other, which is a welcome reminder that it's never too late to have a great marriage.

From a young age, I knew that I loved to teach. As soon as I got home from kindergarten, I would pull out my little table and chairs and direct my sisters to sit still and listen while I showed them what I had learned that day. I taught them all the letters of the alphabet and how to tie their shoelaces.

During the summers, I would invite all the children in the neighborhood to come to my house to be my pupils or do Vacation Bible School with me. I was a strict teacher, and when the situation warranted it, an authoritative principal at the same time. Yes, I loved to be in control from a very young age.

I went to public school with the exception of kindergarten to second grade when my parents put me in a Christian school. I didn't have any close girlfriends until college. Since my mom was my best friend, she would often share with me her frustrations about my dad. This caused me to grow up not liking my father very much, even though I knew there were many fine qualities about him. Despite my mother voicing these opinions with me, which I now recognize was inappropriate, she was a great mom. I loved her very much. She disciplined us when we were young, so we grew up to be fairly disciplined adults. She also fixed us nourishing food and was always there when we needed her since she was home full time. We knew she loved us.

My dad was a good father who loved us in the best way he knew how. He worked hard, was a faithful husband to my mom, and a great provider. He loved the Lord deeply, and we always knew he loved us. We were blessed to have parents who were both affectionate and loving toward us.

While growing up, my family regularly attended church together, but unfortunately the doctrine being taught was biblically weak. I did learn several good Bible stories in Sunday school, but that was about it. My parents didn't teach me from the Bible at home, aside from reading a few storybook Bible stories here and there, but I always knew they loved Jesus because of the priority they put on attending church.

I was exposed to a lot of filthy talk in the public schools I attended and could never find any girlfriends who loved the Lord and wanted to obey Him. All the Christian girls I hung around with looked and acted no different than the rest of the world.

MEETING GUYS

My mother made me wait until I was sixteen years old to begin dating since this was the standard our parents agreed upon. The first guy to take me out drove us to a drive-in theater, where he immediately pushed me down on the front seat of his car, laid on top of me, and started making out with me.

Actually, he made it known, right then and there, that he wanted a lot more than a few kisses. I was appalled! I had never even kissed a guy before and had no interest in what he was wanting to do. I told him to take me home right this instant, and he complied. In fact, he drove me home so fast we almost got into an accident by driving over the center divider.

There were only two guys that I had steady relationships with in high school. They were both great guys, but they didn't have a strong relationship with Jesus, if any. They supposedly "accepted" Jesus into their hearts while we were dating, but doing that didn't seem to mean much to them or change anything in their lives for long. My mom didn't care if I dated unbelievers, but she told us to marry a Christian and not to have sex before marriage. This was the extent of her counsel. Even though my sisters and I all married Christians and were technically "virgins" when we got married, I wish she had provided stricter boundaries for us since boundaries provide security and protection for teenage girls.

My parents wanted me to attend a Christian college after I graduated from high school, and my dad thought I needed to have a career "just in case." This was a bit ironic since he never wanted my mom to work outside of the home, but society had changed and women were being expected to choose a career. All I ever wanted to be was a wife and mother just like Mom, but I obeyed Dad and attended Westmont College in Santa Barbara, California. I made some great friends my freshmen year of college, and we're still great friends to this day. That year, I decided to take my faith in the Lord more seriously and desired to follow Him in every area of my life. I had always loved Jesus up to that point, but I didn't know exactly how He fit into my everyday life.

Throughout my four years at Westmont, I felt that God protected me in the area of male relationships. Every guy I had a crush on didn't like me and every guy who liked me, I didn't like.

Just before Christmas break of my senior year, my roommate, Vicky Alexander, introduced me to her brother Ken. I remember walking with him from the Dining Commons one day and talking with him as we traversed the campus. He was friendly, intelligent, and good-looking, which were qualities that I was looking for in a guy. But that's as far as things went between us.

I remember Vicky telling me one time that Ken had a steady girlfriend in their hometown of Miami, Florida, and he was going to see her during Christmas, as well as the whole month of January during a term break. As he left for the holidays, I felt disappointed because I was semi-attracted to him. Once I found out someone else was in the picture, I thought nothing would ever come of us.

When I went home for Christmas, I announced to my parents that I would never get married. I was so over men! I had dated a lot of guys throughout high school and college, and there wasn't one guy I wanted to marry. I told my parents that my destiny, as I saw it at the age of twenty-one, was to become an "old maid." They gave me all the right responses—"No, dear, we're sure that won't happen"—but that's how I felt at the time. When I returned to Westmont at the beginning of the second semester in February, Ken's roommate, a nice guy named Richard, asked me if I wanted to go with Ken to a suite party.

I decided to give Ken, and guys in general, one more chance, so we went to the party and had a great time. I guess you can say it was love at first sight—or maybe second. He broke things off with his girlfriend back in Miami, and it was full speed ahead for us. We spent a lot of time at the beach, would go out together to eat, and were pretty much inseparable after that.

After graduation, we flew to Miami together to meet his family. I stayed there a month, hanging out and getting to know him even better. I had a chance to meet his family and friends, and he had fun showing me his favorite places in South Beach.

Even though we enjoyed each other's company and loved

being with each other, I noticed that we started arguing fairly often. I was usually upset with Ken about something. Since his parents never argued, he didn't know quite how to handle this. Our relationship continued to go downhill, but on the night before I was supposed to leave for California, he surprised me by asking if I'd like to become Mrs. Alexander. His proposal was matter-of-fact—no ring, no romantic dinner, nothing special. We were just having a nice conversation when there was suddenly a pause. And that's when he said, "Will you marry me?"

"Yes," I replied with a smile, but inside, I wasn't very excited. Because of the constant arguments, a distance had grown between us. We no longer enjoyed each other like we did at college, and even though I said yes, I decided I would still think about it.

Several days after being home, however, I missed Ken terribly and decided I couldn't live without him. I knew I loved him even though I didn't necessarily enjoy him. It was then decided that Ken would come to California and live with my parents and me until our wedding in December—in separate bedrooms, of course. When he arrived at my parents' Canyon Country home, we were glad to see each other, but the arguments continued.

Don't get me wrong: we still had good times. We were also strongly attracted to each other and knew we would make great parents if and when God blessed us with children. That's why I decided to follow through and marry Ken.

WEDDING BELLS

We married on December 27, 1980, and moved into a little trailer in nearby Newhall, California, for the first several years of marriage. I was going to school to get my teaching credential and working evenings as a waitress. Ken was in seminary and found a job that taught orthodontists how to better manage their practices. Through this part-time scheduling work, he learned that he liked working with orthodontists so much that he decided to make consulting his career.

During this time of transition, we experienced a rough couple of years, and the arguing continued to increase. Thinking there was something wrong with me, I read every Christian marriage book I could find and truly believed I was being a godly, submissive wife. After all, I kept the house clean, fixed delicious meals, and gave him *lots* of sex. I thought I was perfect!

But I viewed Ken as far from perfect . . . and I was convinced that he was definitely *not* loving me as Christ loved the church.

Since Ken was going to seminary and working part-time back then, he was a busy guy. Even though he was working hard to provide for our future, I wasn't satisfied because I didn't think he was giving me the praise and attention I deserved. He also continued the poor eating habits he had before we were married, and that remained a *huge* source of contention between us. As I allowed the discontentment in my heart to grow, I found myself constantly battling his decisions and making our lives miserable. Looking back, I would say that I was very unhappy with how things were working out between us, and I even asked Ken, at one point, if he thought we made a mistake in getting married.

In spite of how difficult things were between us, we kept our commitment to our marriage and, a year and a half later, I finally became pregnant. Ken and I were so excited to be expecting our first child, but the excitement quickly turned to heartbreak when we discovered that I was having a miscarriage. All I ever wanted was to be a wife and mother.

Shortly after my miscarriage, we discovered we were pregnant again, and while thankful, we also experienced a mixture of nervousness and excitement. The Lord answered our prayers, and this time the pregnancy went much smoother. Alyssa Marie arrived on May 27, 1983, a year and a half after I received my teaching credential. And to keep things interesting, Ken graduated from seminary on the very day Alyssa was born.

She was a beautiful baby, and I was so happy to finally be a mother. We had moved into an 1,800-square-foot, four-bedroom home in Canyon Country nine months earlier, so, in my mind, we were all set to start raising a family.

When Alyssa was four months old, I had to go back to teaching full time at an inner-city Los Angeles school. My mom or my neighbor, who had a child-care business in her home, took care of her while I worked. This was a painful time in my life; I missed being with my daughter and was always exhausted juggling work and caring for a baby after a long day. That first year, I spent my work breaks in the principal's bathroom pumping breast milk, instead of being at home nursing my baby in my arms. I felt like I wasn't a good wife, mother, or teacher.

The second year, the elementary school a mile from my home needed a first-grade teacher. I knew Sulphur Springs Elementary well because this was the same elementary school I had attended. I also welcomed the chance to get out of a tough situation teaching at an inner-city school, where many children didn't have fathers in the home and few parents came to parent-teacher conferences. My car was broken into three times in the school parking lot in the short time I worked there.

My new elementary school felt like heaven since the parents were involved and the children were well-disciplined.

By the time I started teaching at Sulphur Springs, however, I was pregnant with my second child. My life quickly became increasingly strained trying to manage being pregnant, working full time, being attentive to a husband focused on building his career, and running a household with a one-year-old in tow. I found myself growing more exhausted and sick by the day, and it was only through God's strength that I was able to get by.

After Ryan was born, Ken and I decided that I would stay at home. Ken thought we could make it on his income, so I was able to quit my job. Yay! I never wanted a career. It was always my heart's desire to just be a great wife and mom and have a happy home.

I had two more children after that—Steven and Cassi. When I was pregnant with Cassi, my fourth, I became quite ill. I had diarrhea and was nauseous the entire pregnancy. Soon after Cassi was born, we moved down to the San Diego area. My sister, Alisa, and her family lived in Encinitas, a coastal community, and we loved the area. We made some money on our home north of Los Angeles, which we put into a nice home in Encinitas.

I was still very sick when we made the move in the summer of 1989. After many doctor visits and tests, we finally discovered that I was infested with parasites. Two of my children had the same affliction, so we all took powerful prescription drugs. It took several years to get rid of the parasites, and my stomach has never fully recovered from the damage done by the teeny critters and the potent drugs.

Even though the move was good for us, our marriage floundered. We tried marriage counseling for the first time, which wasn't easy to do, but even meeting with a third party to discuss our problems didn't help. Meanwhile, I continued to read every marriage book I could find, but nothing seemed to help. I just kept reading the part about the man's responsibility in the marriage and thought Ken never lived up to what he was supposed to do.

It seemed most marriage books taught more about how the husband was to love his wife rather than the wife's part, which was "submitting" to her husband. (Submission is when the husband is the head of the wife, and the wife is his help meet in life. I will write about this in detail later.) We even went to our pastor once, and after hearing from both of us, he looked at Ken and told him he needed to love me more. Whenever Ken shared his difficulties with a few close friends, they all told him to just love me more. So Ken kept trying to love me more.

I continued with my efforts to be a good wife and a good mother. I took my children faithfully every week to Awana, which is a children's ministry that helps them memorize the Bible. Ken and I would teach the Sunday school classes that my children were in, and I would read them passages from the Bible as they ate their breakfast. I fed them nourishing foods and took good care of them. Thankfully, my mom lived nearby and helped out a lot.

When Ryan was a senior in high school, he broke his ankle badly during a basketball game. When I took him to the doctor to get his cast off, I felt so ill that I had to leave. My dad showed up to be with him as I rushed home. This event happened on a Wednesday, and I was too ill to even sleep or eat until Friday afternoon.

I finally went to Ken and told him I had to go to the emergency room right away. By the time we got there, I was shaking so badly that I could barely walk from the car into the ER. The doctor on duty discovered that my sodium level was 115, which meant I was near death, since sodium levels are supposed to be between 136 and 146. A CAT scan was then ordered for my body, which had been damaged from all the diarrhea and vomiting.

"Could you do a CAT scan of my head?" I asked. I had suffered through terrible headaches for the last six months and had experienced various head and neck injuries over the years from bad traffic accidents.

On a Sunday afternoon, while Ken was caring for the children at home, a neurologist stepped into my hospital room and told me I had a benign brain tumor. Arrangements were then made for me to undergo surgery at the USC Medical Center in Los Angeles, which went well. During post-op, my surgeon said he had removed all of the tumor and there was only a 6 percent chance of it ever returning. I was thrilled to hear this good news.

BECOMING HIS HELP MEET

During my long recovery, I had the opportunity to do a lot of reading. One time, I saw a magazine article by Christian author Debi Pearl about the three personality types of men. When I showed my mom the article, she was so impressed that she decided to buy me a copy of Debi's book, *Created to Be His Help Meet: Discover How God Can Make Your Marriage Glorious.*

Debi was the first author to open my eyes and knock some sense into me with her convicting words. Up until this time, I had only been focusing on all of Ken's faults and how he didn't measure up to my expectations. What Debi taught me, however, was that I had to do *my* part if our marriage was going to get better; in other words, I had to stop blaming everything on Ken and take responsibility for my wrongdoing.

This was the wake-up call I needed to fix myself as a wife and begin my journey toward becoming a Transformed Wife. As our marriage began to flourish and I developed confidence in my role as a godly wife, I started mentoring other women both individually and in church groups. I loved Debi's book and bought cases of *Created to Be His Help Meet,* which I shared widely. It didn't take long before I discovered that not only did I have a gift for teaching but a true passion for mentoring other women and seeing their marriages transformed.

Several years after I began mentoring, I started having difficulty walking. Waves of pain swept through my body, and this time around, we didn't wait long to get an MRI. When the test results showed no tumor, I had another MRI taken of my neck. This MRI revealed that the disc between C3 and C4 was pushing into my spinal cord. After a difficult surgery to correct this, I braced myself for another year-long recovery.

As time passed, the children grew up, went off to college, and met their future mates. Ryan was the first to marry, falling in love with a wonderful young woman named Erin while they both attended Biola University (a Christian college in Southern California). They were married at a beautiful vineyard in Northern California.

Ryan and Erin conceived my first grandbaby on their honeymoon, which earned them a lot of teasing from others and tears of joy from me. Shortly after Emma was born, Alyssa, my oldest daughter, married Jon. They exchanged vows on a hill overlooking the Pacific Ocean not far from our home. That beautiful day is etched in my memory forever.

With an empty nest at home and a desire to mentor more women, I decided to start blogging about my experiences and begin teaching other women how to love their husbands and children. I called my blog "Always Learning" with a URL address of www.lorialexander.blogspot.com.

When my first grandchild Emma was around one year old, I began feeling terrible again. My head was killing me, and I told Ken I thought something was terribly wrong. I went in for yet another MRI. The next morning, Ken had to leave on a business trip to Florida, so I went to the doctor's office alone to get the MRI results. When the radiologist came out to see me in the waiting room, I knew that wasn't a good sign.

He escorted me to an examination room and quickly cut to the chase: "Lori, you have a mass in your brain."

I sucked in my breath. "Is it in my pituitary region?" If so, I knew what I was in for.

"Yes, it is. It's in the same area as your last one," my radiologist answered.

We discussed how soon the surgical procedure could happen and made plans accordingly. When we were done, I went to the car and called Ken. After hearing the difficult news, he caught the next flight for San Diego and came right home.

I had my second brain surgery at the USC Medical Center, but this time, it wasn't as successful as the first one. The mass in my head was still a Grade 1 benign tumor, but unlike last time, it had a sticky quality to it. Since the tumor was pushing against my carotid arteries, pituitary gland, and optic nerves, the surgeon didn't want to dig too deeply.

In coming months, an oncology radiologist treated me with CyberKnife, a highly specialized form of radiation that was physically and mentally difficult for me to endure. His assistants secured my head to a table with a tight mask while a huge robot roamed around my head, shooting radiation into my skull. I had to suffer through these treatments for five days in a row, fifty minutes each time. My doctor hoped that these series of treatments would control my tumor for the rest of my life without killing my pituitary gland or damaging my optic nerves. Only time will tell if that will be the case.

Through all this pain and suffering, God has been with me, teaching me to rely on Him alone. Experiencing chronic pain can be a lonely experience when the people around you don't know what you're feeling, but I choose to renew my mind with God's Truth. When I begin to panic, I remind myself that I am a new creature in Christ, and that I can do all things through Christ who strengthens me. I know He will never give me more than I can handle.

During the many painful, sleepless nights, I would meditate on hymns or songs of praise, which helped me focus on the Lord instead of on my pain. I knew life on Earth was short, and I wanted to use my time to glorify God and speak truth to others, even when that message would be unpopular.

A few months after the CyberKnife treatments, my youngest daughter, Cassi, married Ryan Boyer. I was still feeling terrible on the day of the wedding, but the Lord answered our prayers that I'd feel well enough to enjoy her wedding day. Cassi got married at the same place that Alyssa and Jon had exchanged vows—the Crossings Golf Course in Carlsbad. It was a bright, sunny afternoon, and Ryan's daughter, Emma, was the flower girl. By this time, Ryan and Erin had another baby they named Kenny.

Steven was my only child unmarried at the time. He was in orthodontic school and would be graduating in August. When he came home for Cassi's wedding, he told Ken and me that he had news to share—he was dating a girl and was serious about her. We were happy to find out that his girlfriend Emily was a godly, amazing woman. They married six months later in her hometown of Houston, Texas. The wedding was in a beautiful church, and the reception was at a gorgeous country club. God is so good.

I'm proud to say that all my children are happily married and three more precious grandchildren have been added to our lives.

LOOKING AHEAD

Now that I've filled you in on my story so you can understand the influences that shaped my life, I will move on to the topic of how you, too, can become a Transformed Wife. Oh, how I wish I had an older woman who would have come alongside me in those early years and said, "Lori, you are not supposed to be treating your husband in this manner. You are called to submit to him and respect him, not try to control him."

But I didn't have that godly woman speak into my life, and for twenty-three years, I tried to control my husband in vain. All it did was build a big wall between the two of us that became wider with each passing quarrel.

The purpose of *The Power of a Transformed Wife* is to help young wives not make the same mistakes that I did. This book may even help older women in difficult marriages, too, since I believe I have discovered the not-so-secret "secret" to having a beautiful marriage, which is clearly spelled out in Scripture. So please join me on this journey as I teach you how God's power can transform any wife's heart.

FROM A POST ON MY BLOG . . .

Michael Pearl and Voddie Baucham, both pastors and speakers, counseled their sons not to marry a woman who wants to make her mark on the world through having a career. Instead, they urged them to find a wife who wants to be their help meet, and who would be hands-on with their children, teaching them and disciplining them full time. To put it simply, they urged their sons to find a wife whose greatest desire was to become a wife and mother.

You see, today's women have been sold a bill of goods. Most young girls aren't being raised to *want* to be a wife and mother. They are being raised to *want* to be like men—independent, in control, strong, and career-minded instead of home-minded. This worldview has wreaked havoc in marriages and hurt children.

Nowhere in the Bible does it tell older women to teach young women to be loud, independent, or career women. God's Word tells us to teach young women to do the following:

1. Love and obey their husbands; being a help meet full time to them. (Titus 2:4-5, Genesis 2:18)

2. Love their children; being with them and faithfully teaching and training them. (Titus 2:5, Proverbs 22:6)

3. Be pure and chaste; having a gentle and quiet spirit, and drawing attention to the Lord, instead of to herself. (Titus 2:5, 1 Peter 3:4)

4. Be keepers at home; where God placed her in ministry. (Titus 2:5)

5. Be good; desiring to be home loving their husbands and children, and pointing them to Jesus. (Titus 2:4-5)

Women in this culture, including those who are Christians, usually hate this message. For me, though, when I finally heard and understood that God's purpose for my life was to be a help meet, it was like a breath of fresh air. I no longer had to exhaust myself trying to be everything to everyone, juggling responsibilities I was never meant to shoulder in the first place.

I know that many women reading my blog feel that same way. They see that God's ways are good and are for the protection of ourselves, our children, and our husbands—*not* to make our lives miserable or keep us from the "good" things in life. As I found out the hard way, all those seemingly "good" things leave nothing but a bitter taste in our mouths.

Plainly stated, Satan doesn't want women at home. He wants them away from the foundation of our society, tiring themselves on less meaningful pursuits, so they are too busy or too tired to please their husbands and teach their children God's ways.

Don't fall for the trap! Obey God. Come home, dear mothers. Come home.

> *Your adornment must not be merely external—braiding the hair, and wearing gold jewelry, or putting on dresses: but let it be the hidden person of the heart, with the imperishable quality of a gentle and quiet spirit, which is precious in the sight of God.*
>
> 1 PETER 3:3-4 (NASB)

2
Why I Mentor Women

The word *mentor* means "someone who teaches or gives help and advice to a less experienced and often younger person," according to *Merriam-Webster Dictionary*.

I have been mentoring women for over ten years. I have mentored women whose husbands were having affairs, drinking way too much, deeply addicted to pornography, lazy and not working, never home due to work, not interested in God, or were absent fathers to their children. I have mentored women through telephone calls, email, texting, my blog, and in person. I love mentoring women as well as young couples. Ken and I have also enjoyed working with a church in their premarital counseling program.

Titus 2:3-5 (KJV) commands older women to teach the "young women to be sober, to love their husbands, to love their children, to be discreet, chaste, keepers at home, good, obedient to their own husbands, that the word of God be not blasphemed." The word *blaspheme* means to speak evil about. As believers, we don't want to do anything that discredits the Bible to those who don't know the Lord. This verse is my calling from God, and I have loved every minute of teaching its truth.

The majority of women today have not grown up with mothers who teach them these important principles. Instead, they've grown up in homes of parents with poor marriages or come from divorced families. They are also being encouraged to go out and get loans so they can go to college, get a career, and then travel and enjoy life before being "tied down" to a husband and a baby—as if these are bad things.

Then, after they have a son and a daughter—if all goes as planned—they have surgery that stops them from being able to have any more children. They don't want to "overpopulate" the earth or have so many children that they don't have enough money for the "necessities" in life—shiny new kitchens, eating out regularly in restaurants, new cars, and the latest tech gadgets.

God tells young women to "marry, bear children, guide the house, give none occasion to the adversary to speak reproachfully" (1 Timothy 5:14, KJV). He also says, "Lo, children are a heritage of the LORD: and the fruit of the womb is his reward. As arrows are in the hand of a mighty man; so are children of the youth. Happy is the man that hath his quiver full of them: they shall not be ashamed, but they shall speak with the enemies in the gate" (Psalm 127:3-5, KJV). The world we live in places a low value on the things God values highly. I always strive to listen to God rather than the culture at large.

In the New Testament, there are many passages that speak about relationships in terms of how we are to behave toward both those in authority over us and those under our authority. These chapters in particular describe how husbands and wives are to relate to each other:

- 1 Peter 3
- Ephesians 5
- Colossians 3
- 1 Corinthians 11

It's rare to find parents who teach their children what Scripture clearly instructs in regards to roles.

Today the topics I teach about are considered controversial, but regardless of current cultural thought, I take the Bible literally. I have found that the more I've learned to be submissive to my husband and a true keeper at home, the better our family life has become. God loves order and has given us women detailed instructions for following His commands so that we may benefit from them. We are wise to surrender to that order and reap the rewards of obeying God's direction.

Contrary to God's Word, I have found that many women in the church—and even many pastors—don't believe in wives being both keepers at home and being in submission to their husbands, which means your husband is the head over you, the leader of your home, and you are his help meet. Instead, they believe in a concept called "mutual submission," which means there is no leader in the marriage and that being an actual "keeper at home" isn't important. Chores such as cooking and cleaning are shared tasks between the husband and wife.

God knows there cannot be two leaders in a home, and He knows that husbands, children, and homes need a keeper to make sure everything runs smoothly. This is why the mother should be considered the "heart" of the home. No one else can take her place. God's ways are not designed to be killjoys or to punish us but are for our own good, to bring happiness into our lives, and to spread the Gospel.

Many women in the church have fallen prey to the

feminist philosophy of being equal with men and achieving everything men do. Women will never be the same as men, and I say this because no one is the same as anyone else. We are *all* unique human beings with different gifts, talents, personalities, and fingerprints. God likes variety. We aren't the same so we should never try to be. Yes, God loves us all equally, and we have equal value in His sight. Jesus came to earth and demonstrated how He values women, even speaking to a Samaritan woman, which was strictly forbidden by the Jews. Counter to the culture of the day, He cared for and taught women of both high and low status who were in need of healing, comforting, forgiveness, and salvation. Jesus died for every single one of us, paying the penalty for our sins, and wants all people to be saved. He loves men, women, and children equally, and He died for all of us so that we might live eternally with Him.

In my counseling experiences, I've found that when women figure out that submissiveness and being a keeper at home is a high calling from God, instead of something to be disdained, their whole attitude changes. They become the joy-filled wives and mothers they were always meant to be. When they figure out they have been misled, or even lied to, by the feminist culture around them, they often have regrets about the path they have chosen. They are quick to get off of the worldly path they were on and jump on to the narrow path that leads to a godly life.

We need to have joyful God-centered marriages and families. We need to reveal the Gospel through the way we live our lives and not blaspheme it, as Scripture warns. There needs to be peace and joy among family members, with wives being their husband's help meets and mothers loving their children by training and disciplining them. When that happens, we model Christ and the Church to a fallen world that desperately needs salvation. If we are living our lives the way we are called to, the world should be able to look at us and say, "I want what they have."

I have personally witnessed women win their husbands to themselves and the Lord through their submission and godly behavior. They learn to have gentle and quiet spirits by allowing their husbands to lead, not being argumentative, and finding contentment in the role the Lord has given them. It is a beautiful thing to witness a wife's frustration, guilt, fear, and shame melt away and the fruit of the Spirit blossom in her life. This is why I love to mentor women in the ways of the Lord.

In the following chapters, I will teach you all that I have learned through God's Word as well as through my experiences and those of others. You won't find change easy, but following God's path makes for a much more glorious journey. So fasten your seatbelts and let's hit the narrow road.

I'll close by sharing what pastor John MacArthur, a well-known Bible teacher, has to say about this topic:

> Women don't want to be workers at home. Why? Because Satan sells the system on that. Why? Because it's anti-God, anti-Christ, and anti-Bible, and it devastates the testimony of the church.
>
> The word "workers at home" is one word in the Greek, *oikourgos*, coming from two root words, *oikos*, which means house, and *ergon*, which means work. It's simply saying that the sphere of a woman's life is her home, and that's her domain. It doesn't mean she has to be there twenty-four hours a day and can never leave. The woman in Proverbs 31 left home when she needed to buy a field, she left home to prepare that field, and she

left home and went afar to find things that would help the family. The woman did what she needed to do, but the focus of everything she did was the home. And since that's the place she poured her life into, she got up early and she went to bed late for the sake of the home. She is to be a home keeper, that's the sphere of her responsibility, that's her place of employment, that's where she should pour her life.

For a mother to get a job outside the home and send her children to daycare is to shirk her God-given responsibility. Ephesians 5 makes it clear that a husband is to be the provider, so even if the woman is choosing employment for a worthy goal, such as sending her children to a Christian school, she is nonetheless operating outside of God's instructed role for her. Better that she accept the boundaries that her husband's salary provides and raise her own children to be godly.

What resonates with me about what John MacArthur said is that women who have listened to the feminists' lies are missing out on God's best for them and their loved ones. Many women have written to me who have come home from their careers and are so happy they did. These women understood that their children's eternal souls were at stake, and they wanted to be the one with their children, teaching and training them full time in the ways of the Lord.

FROM A POST ON MY BLOG . . .

Feminists won because they were able to convince women they had no worth staying at home raising children and being a homemaker. They convinced us that these things were boring and there was so much more life waiting for them "out there"—wherever that was. Women fell for it hook, line and sinker, including Christian women.

A major problem with the way our society thinks is that they assume the only way for a woman to use her intelligence, talents, and gifts is through a paid career. They assume if you don't have a paid career you are wasting your life. They fail to see that a true "help meet" has endless opportunities such as:

- Teaching their children apologetics, theology, and history and reading great literature with them.

- Reading and learning about finances and economics in order to better run the household and the family budget.

- Learning about nutrition and home-healing remedies.

- Exercising their creative talents by baking, cooking, decorating, creating, etc.

- Discussing world events and politics with their husband (and older children) over dinner.

- Being a fruitful member of the household of God by actually having the time to participate in ministry and devote time to prayer.

- Using their gifts and talents to help further their husband's career, whether that means proofreading speeches, entertaining colleagues, or giving wise perspective (when asked) about problems at the office. To say a woman needs a paid career to use her gifts, talents, and brain is such a narrow-minded view of the matter.

It's ridiculous that feminists have been able to convince women that hurriedly leaving their home each morning, driving in traffic, working for someone else from 9 to 5, rushing home, trying to do all the housework, get dinner ready, and falling into bed exhausted each night, just to wake up the next morning to do the same thing, is better than being at home full-time. Here is a great quote from *The History of Womanhood That Feminists Don't Want You to Know* by Anna Sofia and Elizabeth Botkin:

> In Scripture, man's work and woman's work are equally valid—wifehood, motherhood, homemaking, and femininity are not belittled, and women are not guilt-manipulated into living and acting like men.

On the contrary, woman's distinctiveness from man is praised and honored, and her unique role is held vital. Women were to be protected and cherished, to "attain honor" (Proverbs 11:16) and be "praised in the gates" (Proverbs 31:31). It wasn't until the advent of women's liberation that women were told, "Your value as a woman is determined by how well you can perform as a man. Being a woman is no longer enough."

Enjoy being a woman! Cherish the role the Lord has given you. I have always loved being female and feminine. I love that my husband is male and masculine. I love the differences between male and female. We should rejoice in the differences of these roles instead of trying to be something we were not created to be. You aren't wasting your life at home. You are right where you are supposed to be.

* *

Many daughters have done virtuously, but you excel them all. Favour is deceitful, and beauty is vain: but a woman that feareth the LORD, she shall be praised. Give her of the fruit of her hands; and let her own works praise her in the gates.

Proverbs 31:29-31 (KJV)

3
Let It Go!

The first thing you need to do in order to have a good marriage is to *let it go*. You must no longer try to control or criticize your husband in any way.

Ken was a donut-and-pizza kind of guy when we married. A salad, to him, meant some iceberg lettuce, a few slices of carrots, and tons of blue cheese dressing and croutons.

I was raised as a health nut. When I was five years old, my mom developed colitis, which is bleeding of the intestines. The doctors told her the disease was incurable and she would need to take drugs and only eat white bread and white rice for the rest of her life. Even though Mom had been raised by a mother who believed that doctors, drugs, and demons were synonymous, she first tried the drug route, since my dad was a doctor and prescriptive drugs seemed to be the answer to every health problem.

When the medications Mom took made her terribly ill, she no longer wanted to take any drugs. She went to a "health retreat" where the regimen was water only for twenty-one days, followed by organic fruit and vegetable juices. She came home skinny but feeling much better. Unfortunately, as soon as she went back to her old ways of eating, the bleeding returned. She committed herself, from that moment on, to eating lots of healthy organic fruits and vegetables. That seemed to do the trick. After several years of healthy eating, her colon was completely healed. Thereafter, she only had problems with milk products, beef, and chocolate. As a result of her healing, she became committed to cooking only healthy foods in the home and teaching her daughters to value healthy eating and living.

When I met Ken, I was determined to change his eating habits because his idea of dinner was driving to the closest fast food restaurant on many nights. After we married, I was appalled every time he came home from the supermarket carrying brown paper bags filled with root beer, bagels, tubs of cream cheese, ice cream, and potato chips. This made me angry. When we went out to dinner, he would order steak, which at that time I thought was terrible to eat since Mom had taught us to stay away from red meat. To make it clear that I disapproved, I would give him the silent treatment the rest of the night.

Needless to say, our food differences became a huge struggle in our marriage. I would feed my children healthy foods like organic turkey hot dogs, eggs with homemade bread, big salads, cut-up fruit, homemade spaghetti sauce, and various soups I made from scratch, but Ken would sneak them ice cream when I wasn't looking. We were not a united front in this area. I didn't want my children to have any junk, period—no junk food, no junky movies, and no junky television.

I hated being so overly rigid. I cared way too much about stuff like that, which made for a difficult marriage. I'm sure Ken felt like he married a mother instead of a wife.

After I read *Created to Be His Help Meet*, I realized that I had to let some things go, and one of those things was my obsession with avoiding junk food. Once I backed off, an interesting thing happened: Ken began making better choices about what he ate, and we no longer argued about his eating habits like we had in the past.

When I learned not to try to control Ken in how he ate, I felt released from my overwhelming desire to control him in other areas of his life. I realized that he was a grown man who should be allowed to make his own decisions and live life the way he wanted. I no longer badgered him about what he ate, what he watched, how he spent his free time, and how he chose to live his life. I'm thankful I finally came to my senses about this because I sure didn't want someone else trying to control *me*.

I don't know why we, as wives, think we can control our husbands in the first place. I believe it has to go back to the Curse when Eve was told that her desire would be for her husband, but he would rule over her (Genesis 3:16). The word "desire" here means desire to control. Every woman I have ever mentored desires to control her husband in some way through her moods, emotions, actions, or words. This is something you must learn to give up if you hope to have a great marriage.

I believe most men struggle with their sexual nature the same way women often struggle with their desire to control the people in their lives. Our female emotions sometimes push us to control or "punish" our husbands with our behavior when we think they're not living up to our expectations. I still battle this desire at times, but Ken and I have learned to respectfully hold each other accountable when we are tempted by our greatest struggles. Neither of us wants to do anything that is contrary to God's Word, so we bless each other in this way.

For some reason, women (me included) act like we are wiser, smarter, and more spiritual than our husbands. Do you know what the root of this is? It's pride, plain and simple. When you try to control your husband, you're saying that you're better than him. This is not God's way. We're called to have gentle and quiet spirits; to be humble and think of others more highly than ourselves. God's ways are completely opposite of our natural tendencies, but they always bring peace.

When I finally understood this truth, I let go. I put all of my expectations of Ken in a figurative box, wrapped it with pretty paper, put a bow on it, and gave it to Jesus. After all, the job of convicting and changing my husband belongs to Him alone. By letting go, I gave my husband the freedom to live his life without my constant disapproval of him.

Can I ask you to do the same, dear sisters in Christ? Can I ask you to give up all control of your husband here and now and lay it at the foot of the cross? Yes, some of you have husbands with poor health habits—eating too many sketchy foods, smoking, or not getting enough exercise or sleep—and, yes, these habits may result in afflictions like diabetes and heart disease.

What you need to understand, though, is that you can't change him or convict him of these things. You can share your thoughts and feelings with him when the time is right, but then you have to let it go and let God take it from there. Even if his poor choices end up costing him his life, this is a burden you shouldn't be carrying. Instead, spend your energy on being a wife who makes his days on earth pleasant instead of forged in strife. What was ironic, in my situation, was that the more I gave up control, the more Ken became the husband I always wanted him to be.

I can assure you that it felt like a burden had been lifted from my shoulders when I finally chose to let everything go. I no longer had to be responsible for what he ate or watched or chose to do. What freedom for both of us!

Decide today to no longer try to control anything about your husband. If you need to confront him about something, do so in a gentle and submissive way. Don't argue. Say your piece once and then give it to God to convict and change him—and He can do a *way* better job of changing him than we ever could. Ask your husband to hold you accountable for your faults and remind him that he can challenge you when he feels like you're trying to control him again. These fruitful discussions will lead to a more peaceful home and a much happier husband.

FROM A POST ON MY BLOG . . .

Control.

It is the Curse from the Garden. Our desire to control our husbands must stop, and that's entirely possible because we are told we can do *all* things through Christ who strengthens us.

You may have a hundred reasons why you feel justified in trying to change his behavior, but you still don't have the right to try and control him. This is not your job. You were created to be his help meet, not his conscience. Share your opinions with him here and there and then let it go.

He's a man now. He gets to live his life the way he wants to live it. He didn't marry you to nag him. In fact, a lot of men are scared to death to get married for fear they are going to be nagged to death and have to walk on eggshells in their own homes. They feel they aren't going to get to live life the way they want and will have to live with a staff sergeant who tries to control them by giving the silent treatment, withholding sex, or venting her emotions. A true help meet doesn't try to control and change her husband, no matter how right she thinks she is and how wrong her husband's behavior may be. Our job is to love, serve, please, submit to, and obey. That is our job description.

Now, you don't want your husband to feel he has to sleep on a corner of a housetop, listen to constant dripping, or live in the wilderness as stated in Proverbs, do you? He should be able to sleep in his comfortable bed with the air conditioning on. We need to make our homes a comfortable place that our husbands long to be.

Therefore, dear wives, go to work making your husband feel at home. Help him by loving and serving him. Let him see Jesus in you, and this will draw him closer to you and to the Lord. Let go of your controlling nature. Release it today. Let it go!

It is better to dwell in a corner of the housetop, than with a brawling woman in a wide house.

PROVERBS 21:9 (KJV)

A continual dropping in a very rainy day and a contentious woman are alike.

PROVERBS 27:15 (KJV)

It is better to dwell in the wilderness, than with a contentious and an angry woman.

PROVERBS 21:19 (KJV)

4
Allow Him to Lead

Scripture paints a clear and perfect picture of the God-ordained roles and behaviors assigned to each spouse in marriage: for the husband to be the head of the wife, and the wife to obey and submit to her husband in *everything*.

Just as every organization must have a leader to provide structure, protection, and authority, God has appointed husbands to fulfill this role in their own homes. A household run by two competing leaders is one of chaos and conflict, but a household that is in submission to its singular, God-ordained authority, is one of peace and unity. Every role in the home is uniquely different and equally important, but when one position steps on the toes of another, the structure begins to crumble.

Genesis says that man was created first, and that the subsequent creation of woman was for the purpose of lending aid to the man. Most women are either appalled by, or choose to overlook, the fact that 1 Corinthians 11:9 clearly states that man was not created for woman, but woman was created for man. Therefore, a wife's calling is not to "domesticate" her husband like so many wives do today, but to gladly *follow* him wherever he leads.

All throughout the Word there are admonitions not to quarrel, nag, argue, or be in conflict with others. This applies to marriage as well. We must learn how to discuss things with our husbands without having to be right or always get our way. Since he is the leader, he gets the final word. God leads our families through our husbands, and this includes their successes *and* their failures. We must trust God by trusting our husbands, even when they don't fulfill their role perfectly.

Of course, if he wants you to sin—like participate in a sex party with other couples or watch porn with him—you shouldn't do those things. You must obey God above your husband. Few men ask their wives to swing, cheat, or steal, but if they do, you must not follow. Also, if he asks you to do anything that would cause harm to you or your children—like taking recreational drugs or having him drive when he is drunk—you must not do these things either. Seek help from local authorities, church elders, older women, or family members if such a case arises. Don't be afraid to ask for help if anyone is in danger.

Logical reasoning is what men typically use in decision-making, while emotions and feelings frequently drive the decisions of women. Men tend to see the big picture, while women see the smaller details. Men are created to go out and slay dragons, while women are created to nurture their families. Men have testosterone levels between 250 and 850 ng/dl (nanograms per deciliter), while women's levels are between 25 and 75 ng/dl. Men are generally stronger and taller than women. God made them different than us for a very good reason, the most important being that they are built to provide and protect.

Men are called by God to provide for their families. They are designed to risk their own safety to protect their loved ones. Women are called by God to bear and raise children. We are definitely the weaker vessel and need the protection and provision of a man in order to best fulfill our complementary role. A man's body tends to be harder than a woman's body, which is softer and has more curves. These biological distinctions affirm God's roles for the sexes and play a big role in what draws us to the opposite sex. God's plan is beautiful, especially in the area of sex.

I believe we must learn to be joyfully submissive. Just as we want our children to obey us with good attitudes, we must obey our husband with good attitudes. If our children are obeying us but rolling their eyes, complaining and being grumpy, is this true obedience? The answer is no. True obedience and submission requires willing obedience because when you obey your husband, you are obeying the Lord. Our husbands are our designated leaders, so we must put aside our pride and follow where they lead.

God tells us in Philippians 4:4 (KJV) to "Rejoice in the Lord always. And again I say, Rejoice." This highlights the importance of doing everything joyfully, including being submissive to our husbands. It all comes down to a heart attitude, doesn't it? Do you really trust God and, thus, your husband? Or do you only trust in your own way? When you fully understand that your husband is God's appointed head over you, you will joyfully submit "as unto the Lord."

But he wants me to work when I have children. He says we need the income, so what am I supposed to do?

Then you must work. But when the time is right, show him Scripture or chapters in this book that speak about the importance of mothers being keepers at home. After you've made your case, give it to the Lord. Pray that He will convict your husband's heart and change his mind.

Give your heart's desire to the Lord and then obey

your husband. In 1 Peter 3:1, the apostle Peter makes an amazing statement that wives may win their husbands "without a word" as they behold their chaste behavior. The essence of the word "chaste" is without obscenity, pure, genuine, and uncorrupt. It may not be easy at first to keep quiet with a gracious attitude, but trust God and His wisdom. Continue to work on becoming a godly, submissive wife, and let the Lord work on your husband.

In this chapter, God also tells us that we are to "adorn ourselves," which means making ourselves beautiful inside and out, and that includes being submissive to our husbands. The world teaches that we make ourselves beautiful through wearing fashionable clothes, applying makeup, showing off the newest hairstyles, getting Botox injections, or even undergoing breast-enhancement surgery to make ourselves more alluring to men, but God says this about true adornment:

> *Your adornment must not be merely external—braiding the hair, and wearing gold jewelry, or putting on dresses; but let it be the hidden person of the heart, with the imperishable quality of a gentle and quiet spirit, which is precious in the sight of God. For in this way in former times the holy women also, who hoped in God, used to adorn themselves, being submissive to their own husbands.*
>
> 1 Peter 3:3-5 (NASB)

So it isn't nice clothing, the perfect body, expensive makeup, and beautiful hair that is supposed to adorn us, but a meek and quiet spirit, along with submission to our husbands. *This* is what truly makes us beautiful.

THE IDEA OF MUTUAL SUBMISSION

Instead of godly roles for men and women, the concept of "mutual submission" between husband and wife is believed by most Christians and even preached in most churches. This idea comes from this verse in Ephesians 5:21 (KJV) that says, ". . . submitting yourselves one to another in the fear of God."

The very next verse says, "Wives, submit yourselves unto your own husbands, as unto the Lord." Later, the apostle Paul tells us, "Children, obey your parents in the Lord: for this is right." Finally, he tells servants to be obedient to their masters. Paul explains what submission looks like and to whom we are to be in submission to:

- wives to husbands
- children to parents
- servants to masters

If Paul was talking about mutual submission, that would mean parents would need to submit to their children in the same way their children submit to them. This would also be true for masters and their servants. That is not what Scripture is saying here, and nowhere in the Bible does it specifically tell husbands to submit to their wives. The term *mutual submission* has been completely misinterpreted and is damaging a lot of marriages.

So here's a question: If husbands and wives mutually submitted to each other, who would make the final decision? There can be conflict and arguing if there isn't one designated leader who has the final say. Someone has to cast the final vote before arguing and conflict occur, and God says it's our husband's responsibility to lead us. Therefore, wives, if you are still arguing with your husbands, it means you are not being submissive to his leadership.

Ken and I argued for twenty-three years, and in doing

so nothing good was accomplished. Our conflicts made our marriage more difficult and unenjoyable every day. We are called to be at peace with all men and all women, and especially with each other. God is a God of peace. He wants peace in our homes, as well as peace and tranquility between husbands and wives.

When I finally learned that I wasn't supposed to argue with Ken anymore, I had to bite my tongue a lot. I had to learn how to discuss things without arguing. I had to learn to state my opinions and thoughts without trying to force Ken to agree with me.

After finally learning to adorn myself with submission, I discovered what a wonderful place it can be. As I grow older with wrinkles, age spots, and gray hair, I know I can still be beautiful when I have a meek and quiet spirit and I am submissive to my husband. It also helps to stand up straight and be joyful. A smile is the best face lift!

One last thought: the Bible also commands that we are to submit to our husbands in *everything*. The apostle Paul tells us, "Therefore as the church is subject unto Christ, so let the wives be to their own husbands in everything" (Ephesians 5:24, KJV). This teaching may seem awful to you, like it once did to me.

But, you see, just when you think you will never get your way, something amazing often happens. You discover that your husband, especially a husband who has a heart for the Lord, was already intent on trying to please you and make you happy. Now that he is free to lead you as he believes is in your best interest, and the best for your family, he becomes comfortable saying "no," but he says it very infrequently. Your husband becomes the spouse you've always dreamed of having in the first place, and maybe he was there all along, but you couldn't get your desire for control out of his way long enough to discover how much he truly loves you. You will see that doing things God's way turns to bountiful blessing for those who are willing to love and serve Him exactly as His instruction manual tells us to live.

God's ways are so upside down, so completely opposite our natural inclinations. When you learn to obey your husband, even in the little things like when he asks you to run an errand, keep the house a certain way, or whatever else he asks you to do, do it as unto the Lord. When you do, you'll see how much better your marriage can become. When you learn to obey your husband in everything, you are ultimately serving and obeying the Lord.

Give submission a try, and you'll find out what you may have been missing all these years!

FROM A POST ON MY BLOG . . .

Scripture *clearly* teaches the idea of submission in marriage, so I am baffled as to why many Christians are critical of this truth. I think it comes down to if a person wishes to accept the Bible as Truth and walk in obedience to the commands therein.

Whenever a person begins an argument with "but," it completely disregards what comes before it. For example, "Yes, God commands submission and specific roles for men and women, *but* my husband is a terrible leader who . . ."

As you can see, the comment implies that a person's sinfulness or blatant disregard of God's Word somehow negates the commandment set forth.

Additionally, what's interesting to me is that those women who have humbled their hearts enough to submit to their husbands are the ones who have the very happiest of marriages. Their husbands are happy because they receive the support they need in order to financially and spiritually lead their families well. Unlike most husbands, they don't have the curse of having to come home to a woman who is always fighting for control or arguing when she doesn't get her way. There is complete unity and marital solidity in this arrangement, and it's a refreshing dynamic for the both of them. God's plan is always perfect, no matter how much society pretends it's outdated.

Those who reject God's teachings on submission miss out on the joy and growth in Christ that it brings. They hold onto their worldly ways with such ferocity that all we can see is their anger and hatred for the very role for which they were beautifully created.

Ladies, there is so much joy in laying down the feminist myths we've been indoctrinated with in pursuit of obedience to God's will. You can fool yourself about the reasons you don't wish to comply, but God's Word is abundantly clear where that rebellion will lead.

People think that if they do things their own way, they'll find freedom and satisfaction in living life uninhibited. Oh, how they deceive themselves! In actuality, true freedom comes, not from the strangling shackles of self-centeredness, but from the beautiful peace of surrender.

> Wives, submit to your own husbands, as to the Lord. For the husband is head of the wife, as also Christ is head of the church, He Himself being the Savior of the body. But as the church is subject unto Christ, so let the wives be to their husbands in everything.
>
> EPHESIANS 5:22-24 (NASB)

5

What Submission Looks Like

Like I said in my opening chapter, I thought I was a submissive wife because I cooked, cleaned, took good care of the children, and gave my husband lots of sex. Since then, I have learned that submission is *a lot* more than that.

Our husbands need to be our first priority. When I ask women if they are a better wife or a better mother, they *always* say mother. The problem with this answer, however, is that if you really were a better mother, you would make your husband your priority.

You see, the best thing you can do for your children is to love their father deeply and care for his needs. Too many wives neglect their husbands once they have children. We think they are grown men and can take care of themselves, but they still need a help meet. You were created to be his help meet first, long before you became a mother. Children who see their mother making them a priority over their father usually instinctively know this is not right. Sadly, though, they often grow up with a jaded view of marriage and end up repeating the same mistakes in their own marriages.

Being submissive means you obey your husband joyfully

in all things, as I discussed in the previous chapter. Study your husband and listen to him so you will know how to best please him. Find out what foods he likes, what he likes you to wear, how he likes you to act, how he likes you to respond to him, how tidy he likes the home, and all the little things that make him happy.

This long list includes having sex with him when he wants it, which I'll get into further in Chapter 7. We are called to do all of these things because God commands it. He wants us to willingly obey out of love for Him and our husbands, as well as to be an example to the world of Christ and His church. We loudly preach the Gospel to a lost world when we submit happily to our husbands as Christ did to His Father.

The Church is called to willingly submit, obey, and please the Lord. In the same way, we should delight in obeying our husbands, instead of doing so grudgingly and under compulsion.

Submission also means we forgive them easily and do not let any root of bitterness grow. We shouldn't replay their faults over and over in our minds and allow those thoughts to grow into anger and resentment. Instead, we should forgive them and immediately change our thoughts, dwelling upon all of their good and noble traits.

Remember, your thoughts can be transformed by renewing your mind with Truth. *All* of your behavior stems from your thoughts. Therefore, if you continually think warm and loving thoughts about your husband, you will treat him warmly and lovingly. However, if you're constantly thinking how inadequate he is, you're going to treat him poorly.

Learn to listen to and value your husband's ideas instead of mocking them. Even when you think his goals are unattainable, learn to support him. You shouldn't joke that you have one more child than you really do—meaning that you're including your husband in with the kids—because when everyone is done laughing, you have not been a blessing to him, but have been completely disrespectful to him and undermined his God-given role and authority.

You shouldn't expect your husband to live up to all of your expectations. You need to realize that every single one of us is far from perfect. Dwell on the characteristics that caused you to fall in love with him in the first place and be happy for who God created him to be. Don't push your convictions onto your husband or nag him for having different ideals than you. Realize that you're not responsible to create or maintain his beliefs and opinions. Stop playing God in your husband's life, allowing some room for him to learn from his mistakes, and live his life the way he believes is best. After all, he is the head of the family, not you.

I know it's counterintuitive to think this way, but you want God to lead him without you constantly questioning his convictions and motives. Understand that complaining and manipulating him into doing things your way won't produce any true or lasting change in him.

When you correct, criticize, or try to control your husband, you become filled with pride—as if you're more important or know better than he does. You should practice humility and allow the Holy Spirit to do His job. Believe me, He does a *much* better job than you can.

On your journey to becoming a wife who no longer desires to control her husband, you will blow it at times. Apologize quickly, learn from your mistakes, and continue loving your husband without trying to change him. Practice makes perfect!

Before I learned to become a transformed wife, I never apologized to Ken. Now if I speak disrespectfully to him—like in a grouchy or know-in-all tone of voice—I apologize quickly.

Saying I'm sorry has become easy for me now.

Being submissive means you no longer try to control your husband *at all.* Your job is not to control him. God has described what your job is, and it doesn't include managing your man. You're to love, serve, submit, respect, please, and obey your husband because God made him head over you. This is not a position of weakness, but one of strength under control. It takes a strong woman to truly allow someone else to lead her. You can do it! God tells us that we can do all things through Christ who strengthens us (Philippians 4:13).

As we go along, I will remind you of this verse often since it has been powerful in my own transformation. In the meantime, keep this verse in mind so that you won't have to make excuses for why you're failing to obey God when it comes to submitting to your husband.

Remember, He has given you everything you need for life and godliness, and you *can* do all things through Christ who strengthens you.

FROM A POST ON MY BLOG . . .

Ken loves to stand up during worship at church while we're singing. I prefer to sit down since my lower back and feet hurt if I stand too long.

One Sunday, he stood, so I stood up beside him and

asked him if he prefers I stand with him.

Ken smiled and said, "Yes."

Then I whispered why I don't like to stand long. "It hurts my back," I said.

Later, after church, we talked about what happened, and he told me that I was welcome to sit down after a minute or two if I start to hurt at all, but he does like me standing beside him. So I decided I would immediately stand whenever he stands, and if the pain gets too much, then I'll sit down, but I can usually handle it.

Another woman who has a blog with many readers wrote about the time she was at church and her pastor just finished a great sermon . . .

> After he finished, I stood up in my pew and clapped and cheered and woot-wooted and pumped my fists and . . . well, let's just say that my church is *not* that kind of church. And so Jim, my husband, said, "Sit down, honey, sit down." So then I stayed standing even longer than I would have because Jim is not the boss of me and nobody puts Baby in a corner. Submitting to your spouse is not really something we focus on much.

Simply put, she is in rebellion to her husband's leadership by completely disrespecting him. Not only that, but she is even bragging to the world about it. I can picture her pumping her fists in defiance as she cheers her pastor's sermon.

I feel sorry for her husband. Imagine how many friends and family watched her husband beckon her to sit down, yet she defiantly stood, perhaps glaring at him or pulling her arm out of his hand. This was a terrible witness to all the young ladies who may have seen her display willful disobedience and disrespect.

Pride got the best of her. Disobeying her husband made him look weak, as if he was asking something completely unreasonable of her. She didn't care that she was probably embarrassing herself and her church.

A woman who wants to be a godly, submissive wife should have handled it this way . . .

> After he finished, I stood up in my pew and clapped and cheered and woot-wooted and pumped my fists and . . . well, let's just say that my church is *not* that kind of church. And so Jim, my husband, said, "Sit down, honey, sit down."
>
> I immediately sat down. After church, I told my husband I was sorry for acting in a way that may have been embarrassing to him. "That's okay," he said. "I know you were excited, but your reaction was a bit over the top. Thanks for taking a seat."

Submission is *not* weakness. It is only a strong woman who decides to submit to her husband and respect the leadership position that the Lord has given him. Also, if your church doesn't teach submission, it doesn't mean you don't need to submit to or respect your husband. Your obedience needs to come out of your desire to please the Lord, not your church and what they do or don't teach.

Remember, you need to be in the Word daily so you understand clearly what the Lord expects of you, not waiting for your pastor to get it right. After all, most pastors seem embarrassed and apologetic that God would even ask a wife to be submissive, even though it is repeated multiple times in His Word.

You can put this baby in the corner any time because this

is where God wants me. Please know that the safest place for you to be is in God's corner. This is where God has called you to be; standing and applauding for His Word, no matter how much others mock you or try to tell you you're wrong.

God is *always* right! He knows what He's doing. He is our Creator and has given us the written Word on how marriage and family life works. If you choose to live it out with love, respect, and submission, you will have a thriving household that the Lord can truly bless.

* * *

> *But I would have you know,*
> *that the head of every man is Christ;*
> *and the head of the woman is the man;*
> *and the head of Christ is God.*
>
> 1 CORINTHIANS 11:3 (KJV)

6
Easy Conflict Resolution

What do you do about arguing and conflict in marriage? It's simple: just don't argue in the first place.

This is not the message we are teaching in our churches, where conflict resolution is the stuff that marriage conferences and retreats are built upon. Most young couples need to learn how to argue properly, right?

When women ask my opinion about what they should do regarding arguing, my advice is: "Don't." If pastors shared a quick little message of "Don't argue" from the pulpit, they would have more time in marriage retreats to concentrate on what God has called us to do, instead of focusing on human communications skills. Imagine what could happen to your marriage if you successfully stopped arguing even before it begins—by biting your tongue as I learned to do.

Ken and I argued most of the time during our first twenty-three years of marriage. We argued in the car, on our walks, on the telephone when he was away on business, and even in bed after we had been romantic. Then I learned that I wasn't supposed to argue with him. As I became a Transformed Wife, I found plenty of verses in the Bible about not arguing, complaining, or being in strife with my husband or others, so I decided I wasn't going to argue anymore. Since it takes two to bicker, if one stops arguing, the fire of conflict dies out.

When the apostle James wrote about what causes fights and quarrels among us, he said it's because we're not getting our way (James 4:1). If we understand that desire for control and selfishness are the root cause of arguing, then we must stop. In Proverbs, Solomon says it's better for a man to live on a rooftop than with a quarreling wife. When you argue with your husband, you're trying to usurp his authority and consequently disrespecting him. Bottom line, you want your own way.

I used to relish a good fight and arguing was simply my default setting, so when I decided to stop squabbling, I had to keep my words in check. In the past, when I would get into a heated disagreement with Ken, I would expect him to apologize to me. It was not until one day, after reading *Created to Be His Help Meet*, that I told him I would never argue with him again.

Ken just smiled at me and said, "Can I hold you to that?"

I quickly threw out my hand to shake his and said "Yes!" The bet was on, and I spent the next month with a proverbial sore tongue after having bitten it so many times.

From the moment of the handshake, our marriage began to improve dramatically. Ken gave me plenty of room to make my point, but when the discussion went into arguing he would say with a smile, "It seems like you're arguing."

Shoot! I had lost the bet and broken my commitment, so I shot out my hand and we shook again, promising Ken, "I will never argue again."

Okay, I still argue sometimes, but it's a rare thing around our home. Who needs to argue when you can just state your case in a kind way and drop it? Until you are a Transformed

Wife, you will naturally want your way and argue because you love to win.

My best friend, Sandy, has been married twice. Her first husband died of a brain tumor and then she remarried. She says she never argued with either of her husbands and they both adore(d) her.

Here's what Sandy learned: when she has something to say, she says it and then leaves it at that. She doesn't demand her way or insist that her husband agree with her. In fact, she doesn't force her opinion on anybody, which is a big reason why everyone loves to be around her. When she's with her husband, she simply follows her husband's lead. She has decided that their relationship is far more important than being right.

Arguing is ugly and never accomplishes anything. I had to learn to discuss things with Ken without veering into a heated dispute or spewing out cross words. It took some time for both of us to figure out at what point the conversation turned from me sharing my opinions to me trying to get my way. I still have times when it's the latter, but I'm a lot better than I used to be. We live now in peace. Household peace is a wonderful thing!

God wants peace and harmony among the brethren, not the turmoil the world is in. How can we draw others to Christ if we look just like the world? They should be attracted to the peace they see in our marriages, in our homes, and among each other. Strive to be at peace with all men and all women and watch your words. If you stray into "shrew" territory, apologize quickly.

If there is something you just cannot agree on, your husband gets to cast the deciding vote. This is God's prescription for arguing, not mine. The more you allow your husband to make the decisions, the less chance you have of getting into an argument. What I've found that works best is to give Ken my opinion in a respectful tone and reassure him that whatever he decides I will support.

Also, train your children not to argue. Ken regularly told the children, "The Alexanders don't fight!" He said this *before* I became the Transformed Wife, but guess what—what he said worked.

For the most part, our kids didn't fight and argue. When there were "arguments," Ken stressed that life wasn't fair. He said things like, "Yes, it isn't fair that you were born in America with two parents, lots of food, and a beautiful home to live in, while others were born in Africa with no parents and starving to death. Life isn't fair."

My children grew up knowing life wasn't fair, and whatever was the perceived injustice, their grievance could not compare to the many blessings they daily received. They grew up with a sick mom and were fully aware that "life is not fair." Because of this perspective, our children are traveling life with fewer disappointments.

If you fight and argue, how can you teach your children to live at peace with each other? Not being belligerent or argumentative must begin with you, dear mothers. Peace in the home must begin with the mom for a wise woman builds up her home.

Don't count on "conflict resolution" techniques to be your savior. Instead, be submissive to your husband and live in peace. Most husbands treasure peace in their home, so he will appreciate you for this.

A WORD FROM KEN

Not long ago, Ken wrote the following response to a blogger who teaches a form of conflict resolution in which the husband and wife continue to talk about their differences until the one with the best idea wins. In a sense, this means there is no leader and no follower.

Instead of sharing one of my blogs in this chapter, I thought it would be instructive to let you hear what Ken has to say on a topic he deals with daily in his consulting work:

> Lori and I have not only a fabulous marriage in many ways, but we also get to share in the blessings of her blog. Almost every day when I'm not traveling, we'll take a walk hand-in-hand in the late afternoon down to the park. In the past, easy banter seemed to always turn into a series of endless arguments about almost anything, especially what the Bible says. Now we have a lot of fun discussing Lori's blog, the questions from the blog, and other Christians' perspectives on life and godliness. One day a reader asked an intriguing question: "Are conflict resolution tools spiritual or fleshly?"
>
> The answer is far more in depth than one might think on the surface. First, many of the tools the church may teach in Conflict Resolution 101 to premarital couples have a spiritual foundation. Much of what mankind believes are the very best human relations tools were given to us by God in His Word some 2,000 to 3,500 years ago. The Mosaic Law, the Book of Proverbs, the sayings of Jesus, and the writings of the apostles are loaded with great precepts by which the believer is to live in harmony with his fellow man, and in particular his spouse and fellow believer.
>
> It's not unusual when I am trying to counsel

a distraught husband who has contacted me for help with his difficult wife, that one of the first things I coach him on is that he can never expect God to bless his marriage until he himself first starts being a "Christian" to his wife.

That declaration usually gets a defensive retort, followed by the question, "What do you mean?"

What I'm saying is that you cannot expect God to enter into your marriage and to heal it with His power and His Spirit if you do not first follow His clear teachings and do your part. Listen, I'm all for training couples in conflict resolution tools, if necessary, but such tools, even those found in the Bible, are not in themselves essentially spiritual.

Are you saying conflict resolution are fleshly tools and not spiritual?

Yes, no, and it depends! This is where we'll find some interesting discussions. Lori and I believe that far too many psychologists, Christian counselors, and Christian marriage bloggers stop too short when it comes to dealing with marriage issues. They teach tools to resolve conflict that are often not much more than the wisdom the world teaches to improve relationships. Wisdom works for everyone who uses it, but being filled with the Spirit and displaying the fruits of the Spirit, these things are uniquely Christian.

So I have a question for you: Do you ever wonder why so many non-Christian marriages appear to be healthier than Christian ones? Why is it that a great egalitarian marriage (where husband and wife are "equal" and there is no leader) looks and feels healthy to even Christian couples?

The answer is that many non-Christian and Christian couples have discovered the wisdom of how to have a great relationship, which includes how to communicate well, how to argue fairly, how to compromise, and how to be generous with a spouse who's in a bad mood from time to time. These are all terrific tools that God did not leave out of the Good Book as He gives us all we need for life and godliness. Lori and I love God's wisdom, and we know that when we do things the way God tells us to, we reap His blessings. Yet, God's design for the heart of marriage goes far beyond getting along with each other and focuses on what God calls being "one flesh."

So here is where we part ways with the others: I don't see how conflict resolution tools, even those with a biblical foundation, are anything more than a call from God to discipline our own flesh as we "treat others the way we would like to be treated." That's right; the vast majority of conflict resolution tools only become spiritual if and when the Spirit of God is moving in and through the one using the tools. Let me try to illustrate what I mean.

Let's say you and your spouse are in a heated argument or disagreement. I'm talking about an intense, don't-give-an-inch confrontation.

Chances are good you have already walked away from God's Spirit, and one or both of you is walking in the flesh (James 4:1-3). Think about it. As soon as you know the temperature on the argument has passed into the red zone, what do you usually do? If you are great at relationships, Christian or non-Christian, you say to yourself,

"Think, think, think. Don't let your emotions get in the way of your relationship with your wife (or husband) right now." If you go in that direction, you can start practicing conflict resolution tools you have learned.

You might ask for a pause in the conversation to let things settle down. You may walk over to your husband and give him a hug and apologize, knowing that saying "I am sorry" does not necessarily mean you are wrong, but it is a great way to deescalate an argument so you can get the discussion back on track. You may remind your husband of certain boundaries the two of you set up, or hold him accountable for his unkind words, or for not practicing good conflict resolution skills like he promised in counseling.

The list is endless as to what you might do in using conflict resolution tools to get the conversation back on track and to resolve your differences. You might even hear your spouse say something like what a young husband told me the other day his wife said to him: "I know what you're doing right now when you say you're sorry, or when you walk out of the room, and I don't appreciate being treated like a child. You are just trying to manage me with your conflict resolution skills."

If you're still with me and can "think, think, think" instead of overreacting to what I'm saying, then ask yourself this question: *Out of the last ten times when you were in a significant disagreement with your husband, did you use your knowledge of conflict resolution skills in a fleshy way or a spiritual way?*

Easy Conflict Resolution

Listen, I don't want to embarrass anyone here, especially myself, but I can think of too few times where I ever used conflict resolution tools in a spiritual way. It used to be that when conflict came up between Lori and me, I jumped into my highly trained consultant's mode to resolve the conflict without one thought of taking Jesus with me, without one inkling that I needed to be walking in the Spirit. Instead, I jumped right into the flesh and tried to solve the problem myself.

Don't get me wrong; I'm sure God was pleased with the way I handled most of our conflicts. I was generally kind, generous, understanding, and communicative in a non-threatening way, but since I want to keep it real here, I did it all by myself in my flesh, not even thinking about checking in with the Spirit.

There are four major planes or surfaces on which Christianity is lived by believers. The first is the baby Christian who hopefully is in the Word daily and learning the heart of God for his life by training in God's precepts and ways. The second is the carnal Christian whose flesh rules him daily. Although he loves the Lord dearly, he feels like he can never get out of the mud hole that he finds himself in. The third is where those of us who are more mature Christians live each day, carrying out God's desires for our lives and fulfilling his precepts, much like the Old Testament saints did, but also all under our own power and in the flesh.

Finally, there is one final plane to which all

believers should aspire, and that is to "walk in the Spirit." The apostle Paul shows us clearly that there is only one answer that will get us out of the mindset of the flesh and into "walking in the Spirit," and that is to stop trying to do things in our own power. We must stop trying to manage our lives and our spouses with His precepts and wisdom, and instead jump in completely with Him and allow Him to do the mighty work we long for, first in our own lives, and then in the life of our spouse.

Here is the heart of Lori's biblical message as I understand it: when a wife gives up on her fleshly needs and desires, deciding instead to show her husband what a walk in the Spirit looks like through submission, love, joy, peace, patience, kindness, goodness, faithfulness, gentleness, and self-control (Galatians 5:22), then the need to manage a godly husband disappears. Instead, the Spirit of God begins a mighty work in her life and then, if necessary, in his life too.

Having set a foundation here, now let me turn to this key verse in Scripture: "And they that are Christ's have crucified the flesh with the affections and lusts" (Galatians 5:24, KJV).

Tell me again: when you use your conflict resolution skills in the future, will they be spiritual or fleshly? Are you willing, the next time you can sense your discussion is turning ugly, to take all the godly precepts that the church, your parents, and the psychologist have taught you and set them aside for a higher plane of spiritual life, and walk in the Spirit?

So instead of saying "think, think, think" and coming up with one more way to convince your spouse, or manage him, send up a prayer that goes something like this:

> "Lord, this Christian life and my marriage is impossible, at least under my own power. The only hope I have of achieving the oneness, closeness, and intimacy with you and with my spouse is to surrender my will, my fleshly desires, and place them on the cross where they belong.
>
> "Help me, Lord, to speak your words, not mine. Help me to shine the life of Jesus in this difficult moment, leaving selfishness behind and stepping out into all that you have for me to walk in the Spirit."

The world says, "Set boundaries, make sure you're protected, hold your spouse accountable with rebuke when necessary, and manage your spouse well with conflict resolution tools."

Then the church "amens" all of this and even uses great biblical precepts to defend what is regularly done in the flesh and not in the Spirit. I cannot make it any clearer than to say I love conflict resolution skills and teach them regularly to believers and non-believers alike, but they can take a relationship only so far.

Instead, imagine a relationship fully depending on our Lord Jesus, and His Spirit who lives inside of us, each and every moment of the day, instead of relying mainly on precepts. Imagine what type of relationship your marriage could explode into if you fully threw yourself into the loving arms of your husband and allowed him to lead you and love you.

This is our dream for Christian marriages everywhere—that instead of building a marriage in baby steps by managing each other through conflict resolution tools—then both spouses would come to a place of true oneness where the wife can trust that her husband loves her completely and wants to meet her needs without her having to manage him to get there.

Until such time, I encourage you to use your biblical and psychological marriage tools to create a semblance of what God wants in a Christian marriage, but don't for an instant think that there isn't a much higher plane for those who are willing to seek out a true biblical marriage of a loving husband leading a wife who joyfully submits.

Just as there is much more to learning to be one with Christ, so too in marriage there is more we all can learn about becoming one flesh, united with Christ, in a Spirit-filled marriage.

Join us on this journey that goes beyond the flesh and its worldly tools and into the realm of the spiritual. It's here you can leave behind the constant struggle to manage your ways and exchange it for the sacred precepts of faith, hope, patience, and trust, which will show you the path to the truest peace your marriage will ever know.

*However, you are not in the flesh but in the Spirit,
if indeed the Spirit of God dwells in you.
But if anyone does not have the Spirit of Christ,
he does not belong to Him.*

Romans 8:9 (NASB)

7

This Thing Called Sex

Men like sex . . a lot.

God made them this way. Men have ten times the testosterone—aka "sex drive"—than we have.

One of the ways you love your husband is by consistently having sex with the one you're supposed to love and please. You are the only one ordained to be his sexual partner. Others can cook his meals, wash his clothes, and clean your house, but you are the only one, in God's plan, who can fulfill his strong sexual desires. Since God commanded older women to teach younger women to love their husbands (Titus 2:4), I'm reminding you that one of the most important ways a wife can express love to her husband is by satisfying him on the marital bed.

I wrote a post about this topic that contained a comment from one of my friends, who goes by the handle TheJoyFilledWife. She is one wise young woman. I'm sharing her comment here for all of you to read because I couldn't have said it any better. The opening paragraphs are my introduction to her wise words:

It seems the majority of women hate the idea of giving their husbands sex three times a week, yet the majority of men would love to make love at *least* that often.

So how do we come together on this difficult issue? TheJoyFilledWife made an amazing comment on a post written by a man who said that as a husband and head of his wife, he had the authority to tell his wife that she should give him sex three times a week. Needless to say, this comment was ridiculed by women who vehemently disagreed. After reading this man's post and seeing the backlash he received from it, TheJoyFilledWife had this to say in response to him:

> When you mentioned in your post that you, and men in general, would be very happy to have sex with their wives three times a week, I know that the number you came up with is probably toned down from how often some husbands would love to be intimate with their wives. I see that as your way of really trying to help the "once a week and every other week" wife realize that satisfying her husband is more attainable than she thought. Sometimes women psych themselves out by thinking that if their husband had their way, they would be having sex morning, noon, and night. While that may have been the case on their honeymoon, and, true, there may be an occasional husband that would love to enjoy their wife at least once a day, I think that the frequency you brought up would satisfy most

husbands out there.

I can't say I'm surprised that your post received negative comments from disgruntled wives because, sadly, this is an area of marriage that is often viewed as optional or barbaric unless both spouses are "in the mood."

Imagine how quickly marriages and families would disintegrate if we had this standard for other areas for which we are responsible. For example, if we had moms refusing to bathe their children because they didn't "feel like it" and husbands only willing to show up at work when they're "in the mood" . . . or the father coming home after a week of traveling to children who are lethargic and weak because Mommy simply didn't "feel" like feeding them while he was away. Can you imagine the implications? Yet protecting the marriage bed by coming together frequently is one of the most important responsibilities in our marriages; so important, in fact, that it was commanded by God.

I have been asked many times how in the world I was capable of saying "yes" to my husband sexually, even amidst severe morning sickness or the exhaustion that often comes with raising small children.

Honestly, I just made the decision the day we got married that I would never say "no" to my husband's advances. Just as I would never say "no" to a child who needs cuddles, a baby who needs nursing, or a family who needs feeding, I was committed to never reject my husband when he needs to be close to me (yes, even if I have a headache).

Call me crazy, but I took God's command for sexual intimacy in marriage seriously. It really doesn't matter what I *feel* like toward my husband when he comes to me—whether we just had a disagreement and I'm unhappy with him or I'm just not in the mood to be touched—because my actions are motivated by my desire to obey God. Denying my husband his marital right is going against God's clear direction, and I sure don't need to *willingly* choose to sin more than I already do!

As for my husband, he's very gracious and has never initiated intimacy when I've had the flu or, obviously, if I've just given birth. Really, though, the issue of tiredness doesn't come up as a potential hindrance because I try not to show it or mention it at all. I would never guilt my children into skipping lunch because I'm feeling tired, so why try and make my husband feel badly for wanting me?

Fatigue is a fact of life at this phase of child-rearing, and I certainly don't want to allow this time of general tiredness to keep my husband and me from thriving in this area of marriage. One day, the kids will be grown and gone and we will have the home to ourselves again. I would rather keep the home fires burning now, so that we will anticipate that time with much excitement.

I love what the TheJoyFilledWife had to say. Let me wrap up by sharing a Scripture that guides me in this important area of relationship between a husband and wife:

> *Let the husband fulfill the duty to the wife, and likewise also the wife to her husband. The wife does not have authority over her own body, but the husband does; and likewise also the husband does not have authority over his own body, but the wife does. Stop depriving one another, except by agreement for a time . . .*
>
> 1 CORINTHIANS 7:3-5A (NASB)

The New Living Translation of 1 Corinthians 7:3 spells it out in even clearer terms: "The husband should fulfill his wife's sexual needs, and the wife should fulfill her husband's needs."

I have mentored women whose husbands were addicted to porn and had affairs. Naturally, these women had grown bitter and angry toward their husbands who had betrayed them, but this resentment is against God's clear command to them. I must stick to the Word of God and teach them their responsibility is to love their husband in spite of his behavior. If he has had an affair, asked for forgiveness, gone through counseling, and been checked for STDs, then I believe the aggrieved spouse should be willing to forgive her husband for any offense against her.

After all, Christ has forgiven us for every single offense against Him and calls us to forgive others not seven times but seventy-seven times. We are to love our enemies and heap burning coals of love upon their heads (Romans 12:20).

Is this difficult? Yes, but read the Book of Hosea and this prophet's love and forgiveness for his unfaithful wife. As God has forgiven us from every single trespass, we must also forgive wayward husbands since we are to be vow keepers—even if they have not been. Always remember that our great God is known for bringing beauty out of ashes and restoring the years the locusts have eaten. Believe and trust in Him.

In addition, we must focus on ourselves and make sure we are walking in faith and obedience to the Lord, regardless of what our husbands are doing. Who knows if God may use our willingness to forgive and love our husband sexually again to draw him to the Lord? Most men see sexual intimacy with their wife as one of the highest expressions of love.

So let him love you . . . a lot.

And as you love him, find out what he enjoys with your lovemaking experience and free yourself from the things that hold you back from your fullest expression of love. Few husbands enjoy routine sex in the missionary position with wives who never move and never say a word or make a sound. The beauty of sex in a marriage is that it gets sweeter with time.

As you and your husband learn to please each other, by the time you hit your thirties and forties, you'll know just the right moves to really rev his engine. After all, no one else can help him with this important area of pleasure and fulfillment. That's why God gave him you!

FROM A POST ON MY BLOG . . .

*R*ecently on another blog there was a discussion about vacations and sex. The author of the post thought that if families go on vacation, couples should be forgoing sex since they could be in the same hotel room or sharing a tent with the kids. The problem with this type of reasoning is that most men go on vacation to have *lots* of sex with their wives!

The post prompted a lot of interesting discussion, and here are several of the best comments from readers:

From Amy:
Sex is what recharges my batteries. Sex is what makes me feel alive, loved, cared for, and respected. I could go on and on, but I just got the feeling, from reading the post, that what I looked forward to most about my vacations didn't matter at all. Really? Thirty minutes out of twenty-four hours can't be prioritized for your husband? It just didn't sit well with me.

From Robert:
As far as the issue of being in the same room, you need to find a way to be much more creative. Ninety percent of the time there's a way to have sex if it's important enough to you.

Yes, it takes thought, planning, and a dash of riskiness, but if you put in the thought and plan things well, they will never know.

I will just state that I would be absolutely devastated if my wife took this approach of not having sex on family vacations. I'm going to go kiss her right now and tell her how awesome she is because she doesn't let that stop her. Where there is a will, there is a way, even while being discreet.

From Charyse:
The man who said 75 percent of the reason he goes on vacation is for sex, that's sad. I go on trips with my family to get away from the everyday routine, enjoy a new piece of this world, learn something new, enjoy my family, and many more reasons. But sex is not the reason for a family vacation.

From Mark:
I'm that gentleman, and let me say I lay down my life every day for my wife and children. If I'm not at work providing for my family, I'm with them.

Why is it so wrong of me to want to have sex with my wife in Yellowstone? Or under the wide open Arizona sky painted by God himself? I have self-control everyday. I don't spend money on me. I don't look at other women. I don't waste time that I should be spending with my family. They get my life, my thoughts, my sweat, and my blood.

Why is it wrong of me to want to do the thing I enjoy most on this earth when I am on vacation?

From Cindy:
So all this is to say that whether at home or on vacation, sex should be a regular part of our married lives. We have sex all the time, anywhere. We went on a cruise last year and took our two daughters, eight and three. Everyone knows how small those state rooms are on a cruise ship. However, we used the darkness and made sure they were sleeping to get our sexcapades on. We just had to be more quiet than normal.

From Amber:
Bathrooms at a hotel or a relative's house, family shower rooms at campgrounds, fun under a blanket in the dark by

the campfire after the little children are in bed works for us! If it doesn't work out, fine. But my husband feels loved every time I try or even *think* of finding a way to make it happen.

From Amber's husband Mark:
Sex is important to me, so Amber tries to find fun and creative ways to make me feel loved. Amber understands me, and instead of trying to change me or make me behave in a certain way, she embraces who I am and what I need and tries to make me feel loved whenever possible.

In short, if more wives approached sex with Amber's attitude, the divorce rate would plummet. God bless my wife.

I have to tell you that many of the women who commented on this post thought that most men are pigs for having the viewpoints of Robert and Mark. They feel they should be able to go on a family vacation and not think about sex. This makes me sad for the men married to these women. It's important to heed the biblical admonition that your body does not belong to you but belongs to your spouse. The frequency of sex then is determined by the spouse who wants it, not the spouse who doesn't.

As I learned from Dr. Dobson on a *Focus on the Family* radio show some twenty-five years ago, it only takes five-to-ten minutes a day to please your man. If frequent intercourse takes a toll on you physically, figure out another way to please him. Your husband will appreciate the creativity.

My husband wouldn't think about going on a vacation with me without the idea of having lots of sex. Time off and time out for sex are synonymous to him, and we always found creative ways to have it discreetly when we were on family vacations. He works his tail off for us! He is nothing close to a pig but always sensitive to my health issues. Ken is an amazing man of God who loves sex with me, just as most men crave sex with the one woman who should love them more than anyone in the world.

I'll close by repeating 1 Corinthians 7:5 (NASB) here: "Stop depriving one another, except by agreement for a time so that you may devote yourselves to prayer, and come together again so that Satan will not tempt you for your lack of self control."

Notice this verse doesn't include family vacations as an excuse to withhold sex from your husband.

8

Win Him Without a Word

"My marriage is terrible, and it's not my fault. You don't know my husband. He's the problem!"

I hear this complaint all the time from wives who come to me seeking help with their difficult or even sinful husbands. What they sometimes end up discovering, however, is that the issue is not always their husband's wrongdoing. Sometimes the bigger problem stems from what *they* have done to push their husbands away over the years through their disrespect and neglect. Keep in mind that God's perfect prescription for a wife is exactly the same if her husband is an unbeliever, a drug abuser, an adulterer, or a believer who is disobedient to the Word.

What is this prescription?

You can win him without a word by your grace-filled, godly behavior because a woman's most potent voice is not the words that she speaks but the life she lives in front of her husband and children. This approach is reminiscent of the saying, "Preach the gospel at all times, and, if necessary, use words."

That's a good way of saying that we shine the life of Jesus

through our lives, which draws others to us but more importantly to Him. What husband would want to change his sinful ways or come to Jesus if his wife keeps trying to argue him into right behavior? Jesus had a word for people who demand that others act a certain way while acting the way they want—hypocrites.

Women, our words are nothing but cold facts and stark arguments to our husbands' ears if they are not first warmed by the Spirit who lives inside of us. It is our regular prayer life as well the study of His Word that turns our chilly words into warm living waters of grace and love for others to see. Imagine a wife allowing God to take every negative thought captive and transforming them through her heart of submission and love for Christ Jesus. What springs forth is the most potent of sermons about Jesus, powerfully speaking to her husband without her ever saying a word.

This is God's way. This is the way to win the heart of every man. The apostle Peter explains this to us in 1 Peter 3:1 (NASB):

> *In the same way, you wives, be submissive to your own husbands so that even if any of them are disobedient to the word, they may be won without a word by the behavior of their wives . . .*

Look at this verse closely and note that "may be won" is actually translated "will be won" in different translations of this Scripture. It's also worth noting what several Bible commentaries have said over the years:

- *Elliot's Commentary for English Readers*: "The gospel as submissively acted by their wives, without a word said on the matter, ought to convert them. The wife above all, without setting up for a preacher, ought, by the discreet charm of her piety, to be the great missionary of the faith. The tense of the original verb indicates that the scheme is certain to succeed."*Benson Commentary*: "Here Peter wisely intimates to women that the silent but powerful persuasion of a becoming behaviour would be more effectual in winning their unbelieving husbands to embrace the gospel than many arguments, proposed perhaps with heat, for the purpose of convincing them. For when the husbands found what a happy influence the gospel had in making their wives sweet-tempered and dutiful in every respect, they could not but entertain a good opinion of a religion, which produced such excellent effects."

- *Cambridge Bible for School and Colleges*: "The silent preaching of conduct is what the Apostle relied on as a more effective instrument of conversion than any argument or debate."

As you can clearly see from these commentaries, Christian women have an incredible power working inside of them, which is the Holy Spirit, who is changing them into the likeness of Christ. By modeling the behavior of Jesus, a wife has the miraculous ability to win a disobedient husband to the Lord.

The word *disobedient* refers to husbands who are clearly acting in ways that are against the Word of God or who do not believe in Jesus as their Savior. The verse, however, is not referring to actions that don't live up to your own *personal* standards of conduct.

If someone had explained this to me early in my marriage, I might not have fought Ken so hard on things that were really my desire instead of God's. Whether you find that your husband is doing something you simply don't like, you know is unhealthy for him, or if he's walking in sin, you still are told by God to respond to him with godly behavior. It's also vital to understand that this verse is simply explaining how every Christian is to live before the Lord. We have the entire life of Jesus modeling this exact behavior for us around the disobedient mankind He came to save. In fact, God directs us to live this way:

> *Do nothing from selfishness or empty conceit, but with humility of mind regard one another as more important than yourselves; do not merely look out for your own personal interests, but also for the interests of others. Have this attitude in yourselves which was also in Christ Jesus, who, although He existed in the form of God, did not regard equality with God a thing to be grasped, but emptied Himself, taking the form of a bond-servant, and being made in the likeness of men. Being found in appearance as a man, He humbled Himself by becoming obedient to the point of death, even death on a cross.*
>
> Philippians 2:3-8 (NASB)

Don't these verses sound familiar to what God is asking wives to do and be with their husbands? The unique part of His instruction to wives is not the part about submission or godly behavior, but that they are to win him *without words* or forcing the gospel on him.

The most difficult part of the admonition is to keep silent while maintaining a godly attitude when you see a wrong, or feel wronged, by your husband. The reason the Bible tells wives to specifically do these things is because many of them believe it's their responsibility to change their husbands. Instead, wives are to live like Jesus before their husbands, even when they don't feel loved.

WINNING HIM BACK

In the ten years that I have been mentoring women, some have had husbands who were very disobedient to God's ways. One of them was a young woman named Susan whose husband was having a torrid affair. She had two young children, and everyone was advising her to divorce him. The first time I sat down to mentor her, she told me about the affair and all the wrong things about her husband.

The next time I met with her was at her warm and cozy home. Upon entering, I noticed a beautiful picture of her family, including her husband, on the living room wall. I looked closely at the picture and said to her, "You have to win your husband back so that you can keep your family together. I'm going to teach you biblical principles so you can do just that."

Before I tell you how her story ends, I want to give you a little background of what I teach women in her situation.

Many times the women I mentor, like Susan, have already visited numerous counselors, pastors, and psychologists. Since nothing has worked, they're desperate for help. Often they've been counseled to leave their husbands, especially if adultery has been committed.

I hear this a lot: *Lori, I'm thinking of separating from my husband and filing for divorce. He doesn't love me anymore.*

Whenever I listen to those words, I try to help the hurting wife by giving her the long-term picture. I do this by asking a series of questions:

- "What about your children? Do you want them

to have a place to call 'home' as they grow older, or do you want your children to say that they're going to 'Mom's house' or 'Dad's house?'"

- "Do you realize the devastating effects that divorce has upon both young children and grown children?"

- "Do you have the means to support yourself and your children if you divorce your husband?"

- "Who will look after the children while you're working? Will you need to depend upon strangers to care for them while you work? And what type of job will you be able to get?"

- "Do you realize that your husband will no longer be sanctified by your presence if you divorce him?"

- "Do you believe God has the power to save your marriage and perform a miracle?"

It's important for you to keep the family together as long as possible because your family is sanctified when you live out a godly life in front of them. When you're not around, Jesus is not there, but when you're in the home with your children and your husband, Jesus is there living inside of you. This dynamic changes after a divorce because you're no longer all under one roof.

Another point to consider is that when your children are at their dad's place, you will have no clue as to what they're seeing or doing. Even though your husband is in a pit—often from adultery, alcoholism, or pornography—his greatest chance of being freed is through your faithfulness in allowing Christ to shine His light through you. He needs you by his side to help him break his bondage to sin. Keep his eternal soul in mind, and this will help you maintain the right perspective.

Read 1 Peter 2 carefully to acquaint yourself with the sufferings of Christ. As Christ has suffered for our sins to save us, "likewise" wives may have to endure difficult times to be a godly witness to their wayward husbands. Suffering is a good thing when it's done for God's glory, as 1 Peter 2:21 (NASB) says:

> *For you have been called for this purpose,*
> *since Christ also suffered for you, leaving you*
> *an example for you to follow in His steps.*

When you're finished reading 1 Peter 2, go on to 1 Peter 3:1-6 for encouragement. After you've stayed close to your husband's side during his rebellion, there's a good chance that he will some day "arise up and call [you] blessed" (Proverbs 31:28, KJV). Your husband will be thankful that you helped pull him out of the pit and that you refused to allow your marriage and family to be destroyed by his sin.

Following the example of Jesus during difficult circumstances is a powerful testimony to a fallen world. I have witnessed the miraculous impact of submissive and godly wives on difficult, disobedient husbands trapped by adultery. Some are still a work in progress, but many others have experienced a glorious reconciliation and healing that they say was worth every heartache and pain.

Even those who were counseling these women to divorce the "scumbag husband" are in awe of the power of God's Word to bring healing to broken marriages and lives. You have the power to preach the gospel louder than most pastors can preach it, with two lives having been transformed through obedience to God's Word.

When that happens, you will be able to share with others how obeying the Lord's commands healed your broken marriage. The simple prescription to be like Jesus toward others can resurrect some of the most difficult relationships. As Scripture reminds us: "And we know God works all things together for good to them that love God, to them who are the called according to His purpose" (Romans 8:28, KJV).

Now, I know many of you may say that a woman with a husband who is an adulterer has clear biblical reasons to divorce him, but what God has joined together, let no man tear asunder. If we are told to forgive someone seventy times seven and love our enemies, how much more should we forgive a disobedient husband, even if it's his seventh transgression? If you want a clear example of God's view on dealing with adultery in marriage, read the Book of Hosea. This Old Testament prophet married a woman who continued her prostitution, yet he stayed faithful to her until the end, just as the Lord stays faithful to His Church.

Now let me get back to what happened to Susan, whose husband was having an affair. Over the next few months, after I explained to her how a godly woman should behave, she transformed herself with the help of the Spirit into someone who became attractive to her husband. Instead of showing disgust toward him, she displayed kindness and warmth. She modeled the gospel to her wayward husband with joyful confidence, knowing full well that no matter what happened, she could stand before the Lord one day with the knowledge that she trusted in Him and remained obedient to His Word.

Few words were spoken between Susan and her wayward husband, but her life became a hook that few men could resist latching on to. After all, what most husbands really want is a joyful wife who is at peace with both him and herself.

Within six months, Susan's husband broke off his affair and asked to reconcile with her. Shortly thereafter, I recall getting a text from Susan in which she told me how thrilled she was that he was attending church with her. What was hardest to believe was that within a few months after that, he was teaching others in his small Spanish-speaking church about a forgiving God who had matched him perfectly with his forgiving help meet. They have been a reunited family for more than six years now.

The most important quality in winning back a husband is a willing and teachable heart. There must be no stubbornness or pride. You must allow the Holy Spirit to do His work inside of you by committing yourself to prayer and reading the Bible daily. Memorize verses that apply to having a quiet and meek spirit. Buy the book *The Ornament of a Meek and Quiet Spirit* by Matthew Henry and study his teaching. Focus on the good in your husband, and every time a bad thought comes into your head about him, throw it out and take it captive to the obedience of Christ.

Remember, the real fight is not with your husband:

> *For our struggle is not against flesh and blood, but against the rulers, against the powers, against the world forces of this darkness, against the spiritual forces of wickedness in the heavenly places.*
>
> EPHESIANS 6:12 (NASB)

To succeed, you must put on the full armor of the Lord (Ephesians 6:10-18). Cling to the Lord's promises when you feel weak during the battle and continue to keep your mind on things above. Imagine your husband as a gift in a box with a bow on top and give him to the Lord.

Concentrate on becoming the godly woman that the Lord has called you to be and allow the Spirit of God to do His work of exhorting, encouraging, and convicting your husband. Angry and resentful words will never compare to the transforming power of our Heavenly Father.

Part of winning your husband is being in subjection to him. Therefore, you must submit to and obey him, unless he asks you to participate in his sin. You will never know what a huge influence these actions have upon him, but the Lord does and will use them for good. It won't always be easy trusting the Lord to do what He's told you to do, but no one can improve upon the formula He gave specifically to women to win back their husbands. Hang on tight to this promise.

If you must separate from him for a time because of his behavior, then so be it, but continue to be kind and loving toward him. Pray for him continually by casting your cares upon the Lord, for He is your strong tower. The Lord hears your prayers and promises that "the effective prayer of a righteous [woman] can accomplish much" (James 5:16, NASB).

Listen, women, I want to share a secret with you: Men are not that complicated. What they want and need most from their wives is respect. Often, affairs happen because their wives are not respecting their husbands at home, or worse yet, in public. If God hadn't built them to need respect, He wouldn't have commanded that wives respect their husbands. In fact, in the King James Version, the word "reverence" that's used in the text can be translated "awe."

Furthermore, the apostle Paul tells us in 1 Peter 3:6 (NASB): "Just as Sara obeyed Abraham, calling him lord, and you have become her children if you do what is right without being frightened by any fear." Therefore, we are not only to reverence our husband but also obey him. Sara showed this reverence to Abraham by calling him lord! We are reminded not to do this in fear, but to trust in the Lord as we follow and respect our husbands.

Some will accuse me of condoning abuse since, in their minds, a wife's desire for submission always leads to abuse. On the contrary, a woman who is kind and gentle to her husband, seeking to please him, will more than likely draw him to herself instead of making him angry enough to abuse her. Self-control is a powerful fruit of the Spirit, and we are called to exercise self-control in every relationship, *especially* with our spouse. It takes a lot of strength to be a woman like this, and it is a weak woman who gives into her emotions and is led astray by her feelings.

God does not ask a wife to submit to abuse, but too often the word abuse is used so frivolously that it does a disservice to those women who are truly abused. It's the degree or method of control that determines whether behavior is truly abusive or simply bad behavior.

The godly woman discerns when it's time to seek help, request counseling, or even go to the authorities when a husband crosses the line from bad behavior into physical or emotional abuse. Don't ever let others tell you that submission is weakness, nor let anyone tell you that submitting to a husband "in everything" means allowing real abuse.

If you are truly showing love, respect, and submission to your husband and you can never please him, keep trying and praying anyway. But if his control becomes overbearing and abusive, it's certainly fine to seek out a counselor or a pastor—or even the police in the case of physical abuse. Check your heart first, but be strong in the Lord in both your desire for godly submission and the desire to please the Lord by keeping yourself and your family out of any danger from any physical abuse.

So consider this: It takes no strength at all to vent your angry thoughts and pour disrespect upon a husband, but for some reason, we are led to believe that treating a husband with love and respect will cause him to abuse us. I don't think so! God will not be mocked! If you think submission automatically leads to abuse, you are listening to the whispers of the enemy. Submission is anything but weakness, and God is not asking you to be vulnerable to abuse but to be strong in the ways of the Lord Jesus.

If a wife's greatest desire for marriage is having a husband who listens to her and gives her a gentle word and loving touch, then a husband's desires are filled by a wife who is respectful and sexually available to him. Most husbands function best when we take good care of them by giving them delicious food and paying attention to the little things—occasions when we joyfully fulfill our role as their help meets. Meet your husband's desires while focusing on becoming the godly woman that the Lord has called you to become, for it is in living out God's design for marriage that a wife finds her innermost needs satisfied.

ANOTHER STORY OF RECONCILIATION

I remember the first day of a women's Bible study at my church. We began by telling each other our names and something about ourselves. One woman named Elizabeth didn't miss a beat in describing what was going on in her life. Elizabeth began to cry as she explained that she and her husband, Jim, were raised in the church and had four children, but her marriage had crumbled when her husband moved out.

I went up to her afterward and asked her if she has ever been around a godly marriage or been mentored by an older woman.

"Neither," she replied between sniffles.

"Would you be open to having me mentor you?" I asked.

"Sure," she said. "I'd welcome that."

The first time I met with her, she told me all the things that were wrong about her husband, Jim. Thankfully, there was no pornography or adultery involved, but there were plenty of other complaints she had about him.

I listened and commiserated with her, and then explained the concept of being a godly, submissive wife and winning Jim without a word. Elizabeth began practicing these principles whenever her husband came to see the children. She started being kind and gracious toward him, dressing attractively when she knew he would be around. She stopped being angry with him and complaining about him to others. She became joyful in his company and even smiled at him. Often, as he left, when the door shut behind him, she would fall to the floor in a heap of tears, but she never cried in front of him.

A few months went by when, one day, Elizabeth asked her husband if he'd like to join her and the children on a beach outing. Jim said yes. While they sat on the sand and watched the children frolic in the surf, Elizabeth began to share with him the many things she now could see she had done wrong to tear their marriage apart through her bad attitude and behavior. With tears streaming down her face, she shared how sorry she was and asked him to forgive her. Her husband then began to confess his part in the destruction of their marriage. The dam that was preventing reconciliation was broken that day as they both wept and clung to each other.

After they acknowledged their shortcomings and both repented of their actions, they agreed that Jim could move back home and resume their marriage on much more solid ground. Elizabeth now has a new perspective on marriage and is determined to follow an obedient walk in the Spirit and no longer live for the flesh. Elizabeth won her man back with very few words and by allowing Jesus to live in and through her by her obedience to His Word. In the end, not only did Elizabeth win, but her family won and, ultimately, so did God.

I stopped meeting with Elizabeth after her husband returned home. A couple of years later, Ken and I were attending a large evangelical church with multiple services when I happened to see her there one morning. She was with her husband, whom I had never been introduced to. Our eyes met with a smile, and when the service was over, she came over and gave me a big hug.

"How are you doing?" I asked.

"Oh, you wouldn't believe it," she gushed. "Jim and I are doing so well. I can't tell you how much you helped me. You literally saved our marriage and changed our lives. Thank you for being such a great mentor to me."

That was humbling to hear after investing so much time and energy to walk her through Scripture and show her what God desires for a godly wife. In all honesty, though, was it really *me* that saved her marriage?

Hardly. God is the one who does all the work and gets all the glory. All we can do is be faithful partners in His plans.

LEAVING A PLACE FOR HIM

Several years ago, I read a book by a godly, praying woman named Connie Hultquist.

Connie is a mother to six children with a husband who was in and out of jail for many years. She prayed continually for his salvation and always set a place for him at the table. She would tell her children that their daddy would return someday. He did return once in a while between jail stints, but it was never pretty.

Eventually, through Connie's steadfast devotion and prayers, her husband finally came home for good. He repented of his evil deeds and came to know the Savior of his soul. They lived a few good years together until he died from a heart attack. You can find her book on Amazon and read her incredible story about never giving up hope of winning her wayward husband without a word. It was her prayers and deep faith that kept her going.

I'm reminded of what pastor Michael Pearl said: "No man has ever crawled out from under his wife's criticism to become a better man." If you think you can change your husband's behavior by being angry with him, giving him the silent treatment, or being bitter toward him, think again. This is not God's formula for winning your husband.

A woman who goes by the moniker of Sunshine Mary had a very wise blog in which she once wrote this:

> You know, ladies, it ultimately does not matter if you are in love with your husband, if you are attracted to him, or even if you are happy with life in general, though certainly these are nice things to have. Despite what you may have been taught, your personal happiness should not be your greatest earthly priority. As a woman of God, you should

never trust your own deceitful heart to lead you. If you are a mother and you actually love your children, you will not do anything to jeopardize their chances of growing up without their father in the home. Instead, you will obey God, take up your cross, and follow Him.

Rather than allowing the world to influence us to prioritize our own happiness above all else and seek fulfillment in the lusts of the flesh, let us remind ourselves of what God calls women to be: faithful, godly, reverent, loving, gentle, kind, selfless, patient, pure, wise, and self-controlled. And if you were blessed enough to have a mother who embraced the cross of self-sacrifice to raise you, take a moment to thank our Lord for her.

A STEADY REMINDER

If you continue reminding yourself that the purpose of life is not to seek pleasure or fulfillment but to do everything for the glory of God, you will have the patience and endurance to stay with a disobedient husband, praying consistently for him to repent from his sin and turn to God.

You must always keep straight your motivation. You win him back by living the way God calls you to live, even when you see no progress on his part. Your love for God and your responsibility to godliness should never be determined by what your husband does or does not do. Instead, your motivation should be based on your love and faithfulness to our Lord Jesus.

Indeed, the believer enters into many promises when we choose to do things God's way. The wife who changes so that she will see change in her husband fulfills a worldly approach that any secular counselor might teach a spouse trying to improve a marriage. Of course, God's ways work best. God commands you to have faith in Him and His promises and to be obedient to His direction, even when you don't see immediate results. So how long must you keep trying to be the person God calls you to be by modeling the godly, gracious, and servant heart of Jesus?

Actually, that's the wrong question. Instead, why would you ever *stop* doing the right thing, whether the situation is with a wayward husband, a cranky parent, or an unfaithful friend? Is your love and obedience conditional, or are you not complete in Him?

The best answer is how long would you want your husband to put up with *your* sins and disobedience if the shoe was on the other foot? Is there a time limit to your husband giving up on *you?* No, because God sets no limits on His love for us, and His love is exactly what the covenant of marriage is all about.

If you have helped turned one person from destruction, here is your promise:

> *Let him know that he who turns a sinner from the error of his way will save his soul from death and will cover a multitude of sins.*
>
> JAMES 5:20 (NASB)

It is worth the cost, dear wives. Yes, the narrow road is not easy to travel. You are called to make continual self-sacrifices and love for others, regardless of the price to you.

If you are a wife whose husband needs Jesus to work mightily in his life, I pray that God will grant you the strength to do everything you can to help your husband get freed from Satan's grasp. Don't give up. Take things one day at a time. Ask God moment by moment for His wisdom and mercy to fall upon your husband and your marriage.

FROM A READER OF MY BLOG . . .

I want to share a testimony from TheJoyFilledWife. She wrote the following post for my blog about her husband's addiction to pornography:

> I don't think I'll forget the date as long as I live.
> It was Sunday, June 2, 2013, when I awoke in a panic, grabbing my smartphone as the chirp of a new email sounded. I quickly cleared the various texts that had piled up over the past several hours and worked on deleting the last of my emails.
> Drawing closer to the final message, I suddenly felt a pit in my stomach sink like a 1,000-pound lead weight. As my eyes fell upon the title of my final email, I knew in my heart that I was about to come face-to-face with one of my greatest fears in life.
> It was the weekly Internet accountability report my husband and I had subscribed to since we got married four years prior. The title of the email urged me to check the content report of the websites

that had been visited in recent hours, stating that there was cause for concern.

Lord, please, anything but this.

With all the courage that I could muster up, I swallowed hard and clicked. In a matter of moments, I felt the air escape from my lungs. Hours upon hours of pornographic image searches. I felt my heart crumble into a million pieces as I sunk my face deep into my pillow to silence my cries.

Please, Lord, don't let this be true. But I knew in my heart that this was no mistake.

I would be lying if I said that I hadn't battled the urge to send the email straight to the trash without opening it. If I did, perhaps I could pretend I never saw it and go on with my life as I knew before. When we go through tragedies, sometimes our first instinct is to pretend it's not happening, especially when we can't make sense of it all, or we want to ask why the Lord would allow us to face such heartbreak.

Yet we serve a God who gives us the courage to fight those tragic battles with our head held high and peace in our heart. Peace amidst trials is nonsense to the world, and, believe me when I tell you, these tragic times are often the greatest opportunity of our lives to show the world the One who dwells within us.

The Lord has called us for such a time as this. If we keep our hearts set on the promises of His Word that "He will never leave us or forsake us" (Deuteronomy 31:6), He will use us to impact more hearts that we can imagine. When we choose joy in the midst of our painful circumstances, it is a powerful testimony to those who are watching from the sidelines. And trust me when I say, there are *always* people watching from the sidelines.

Although my husband is a believer, I knew it would take an act of the Holy Spirit for him to overcome his addiction and subsequent struggle with anger and control. Still, 1 Peter 3:1-2 kept rising up in my heart, that if I submitted myself to my husband, even if he was disobedient to the Word, then he would be won over by how I acted.

If unbelieving husbands can be won over through the behavior of their wives, could the Lord use me in the same way to point my believing husband back to Him?

Lust is often a lifelong battle for men and we, as wives, can lift up our husbands by being their greatest prayer warrior, meeting their physical and emotional needs, being patient with them, and by showing them respect in all areas, unless they ask us to sin. We serve a God who changes hearts, and there is no heart too hard for Jesus to soften.

I pray we will allow Him to use us to minister to our husbands in *all* areas. Before I wrap this up, I feel compelled to say something very important to you fellow wives out there who were or are currently facing this same kind of heartbreak in your marriage:

You are beautiful.

You are valuable.

You are precious.

You *are* good enough.

Not because of who you are, but because of Who you belong to. You are the daughter of the

King. He made you just the way He wanted you and desires to use you to accomplish great things for His Kingdom. Please don't believe the lies of the enemy that tell you if only you were prettier, or taller, or shorter, or thinner, or tanner, or sexier, or better in bed, then your husband wouldn't have made the choices he has.

While we are responsible to fulfill our wifely role and to not cause our husband temptation through neglect or disrespect, we are *not* responsible for their sin.

When our husbands have a stronghold in their lives, the one and only person who can break that bondage is Christ. Hold on to Jesus, for He is "the author and perfecter of our faith" (Hebrews 12:2, NASB). Do not give into fear, sweet sisters, for our precious Lord reminds us, "In this world you will have trouble. But take heart! I have overcome the world" (John 16:33, NIV).

It was a little over a year ago that I faced the most devastating battle of my life and marriage. The countless tears I have cried in the past year have given me a perspective I wouldn't have gained otherwise. Although I prayed for many years that Jesus would strip away the strongholds in my life, I never thought He would do it all at once—and while fighting to survive another day and not give into feelings of hopelessness.

But I have learned so much about the beauty of forgiveness and the power of prayer in the past year, and, although I would never want another human being to have to endure what I have, I know that there are countless others out there who are facing this same battle. Please know that you are not alone.

Perhaps one of the most important lessons I've learned in all this is that joy is not a feeling, but a choice. By the grace of God, my husband is overcoming his addiction, and he has told me countless times what a gift my prayers and patience have been through it all.

Although he still battles his habits and earthly temptations, we are rebuilding trust every day. God is so faithful to walk beside us down this road.

9

Teaching and Training Children in the Way They Should Go

God tells us in His Word that one of your purposes is to raise godly offspring (Malachi 2:15). If you have been blessed with children, part of being a Transformed Wife is training your children in the ways of the Lord so that they have the potential to be transformed by the power of His word. Believe me, there is no greater joy than raising children who walk in truth.

Ken and I have two sons and two daughters. They are all grown up and happily married. We have five grandchildren. All of our children walk in God's truth (3 John 1:4). None of them rebelled from the Lord, which we are grateful for since there is no greater joy than knowing our children are walking with the Lord.

Many considered us strict parents. Since we didn't want "terrible twos" or rebellious teenagers, we knew we needed to teach them obedience at a young age. When they had their first tantrum, we dealt with it right away. Yes, we spanked our children. We spanked them whenever they were disobedient. We took the verses in Proverbs about using the rod on our children seriously and literally.

We always spanked them on their bottoms with a few hard swats with a small strap. When they were really little and still crawling around and put their fingers somewhere that could hurt them, we smacked their fingers and said, "No!" They learned quickly what they could touch and what they could not touch.

Pain is a great teacher. God disciplines us for our good, and we disciplined our children for their good. When we could reason with them and they disobeyed us, we would send them to their room, where we would talk to them in private about what they had done and then give them a few swats on their bottoms. Afterwards, we would hug them and tell them we loved them. (See Proverbs 22:15 and Proverbs 13:24.)

Ken and I insisted they obey us the first time we asked them to do something. Delayed obedience is still disobedience. It was exhausting keeping after them when they were small, but we didn't have to spank them often after they were five years old; even by three years old they were mostly trained to obey us. This happened because we were consistent.

We never had to count 1-2-3 or ground our children. When they were young and whining, emotional, or just in a bad mood, we would send them to sit somewhere all alone until they could get themselves pulled together and behave. We always dealt with misbehavior right away and didn't let things fester. We wanted to train them up in the qualities of the Holy Spirit—love, joy, peace, patience, peace, kindness, and goodness. They weren't going to learn these attributes on their own. We knew it was our responsibility to teach these attributes of godly character to them.

I remember asking Gina, a friend of mine who raised several amazing children, what her secret was. Gina said she and her husband also spanked their children, and then she added this:

We only spanked our children if they disobeyed us and never in anger. If they were somewhere such as a park and it was time to leave, we would tell them that we were leaving in five minutes. In five minutes, we would tell them it was time to go.

All of our children came immediately, to the amazement of all of our friends, who had to count to ten over and over again, raise their voices, and threaten punishments that never came. Then these parents wondered why their children never obeyed them. The reason is that their children never believed them because "no" didn't mean "no."

We also worked with their attitudes. Ken and I wanted our children to obey us with good attitudes since this is how we wanted them to obey the Lord—with a positive outlook. Since God tells children to obey their parents, we must be diligent in teaching them to obey us, and that starts with teaching them to listen to our voice. As soon as you call your child's name, teach him to look at you and say, "Yes?" In this way, you know you have his attention.

We never had one principal, teacher, coach, Sunday school teacher, or anyone in authority ever call us about our children's misbehavior. I knew raising well-behaved, obedient children was possible, or God would not have made that a qualification for becoming a church elder and deacon. Yes, it takes time to raise well-behaved kids, but it was worth it. Child-raising was a joy for us instead of a burden.

We were also careful with the influences in their life. For instance, we didn't allow sleepovers. We wanted them under our roof at night since we had no idea what other parents allowed their children to watch on television or what music they listened to. We didn't allow them to go to most movies with their friends. We didn't allow them to date in high school, but they were welcome to hang out in groups. We wanted to protect their purity and not give the enemy a foothold into their lives.

The Deceiver will take what he can whenever he has a chance, so parents must be wise about what can lead their children into evil and protect them from it. We needed to know who they were hanging out with at all times. Bad company corrupts good morals, and the wise walk with the wise. We took the biblical admonitions seriously and expected our children to as well.

SWEET DREAMS

Ken and I trained our four children to sleep through the night when they were several months old because waking up every few hours took a huge toll on my health and emotions. It was difficult letting them cry at first, but we could distinguish what they wanted by the sound of their cries. When they cried or had trouble sleeping, we would check on them once in a while and pat their back to let them know we were there. After a week or so of this, they became very good sleepers.

We would make sure our babies were well-fed, warm, and dry before putting them in bed for the night. I know that mothers hate letting their babies cry—I get that. The truth of the matter is that not getting enough sleep can greatly hurt *you* as a mom. Rest is imperative for the health of a mother, so the sooner babies learn to sleep through the night, the better.

Everyone wakes up several times a night, even as adults, but we learn to go back to sleep. Babies need to be taught this as well. I know many women disagree with this approach and even tell me my advice causes neurological and emotional problems. Some even accuse me of being selfish! But consider what another mommy blogger had to say:

> Postpartum hormones, six months of sleep deprivation, the neurological impairment it engendered, and the adrenal response of my exhausted body to prolonged stress—this is what rendered me a weepy, terrified mess, staring teary-eyed into the frightened eyes of my children. I had to go on antidepressants.

Reading about her experiences became a light bulb moment for me and caused me to wonder if most of the postpartum depression that women experience today is from not getting enough sleep.

Dr. Bob Marshall, a certified clinical nutritionist and host of the *Healthline Live* radio show, teaches that we need five solid hours of uninterrupted sleep without raising our heads above our chests for the adrenal glands, which produce hormones that repair and replenish the body every night. Because the adrenal glands are absolutely vital to our well-being, I know that a lack of sleep greatly suppresses the adrenal glands and the immune system, thus making one more susceptible to getting the flu, a cold, autoimmune diseases, or even cancer.

When each one of our children started sleeping through the night along with the rest of the house, this made the daytime hours much easier for me. Babies can be trained at an early age to sleep through the night if you want them to, and you can endure a week of a crying baby. Getting through that week was well worth it for us, and today all four of my children are happy, secure, and well-adjusted adults.

Another thing: we never allowed them to sleep in our bed with us. Aside from the attachment issues, most of the women who allow their children to sleep in their beds do so against their husband's wishes. Most men want their wives to themselves in bed. Women must always remember that they were created first to be their husband's help meets, and they were this way before they were mothers. The greatest gift they can give their children is to love their husbands deeply and make them a priority in their lives. If your children do sleep in your bed, make sure it is your husband's idea and not your own.

As our children were growing up, they went to church with us every week and also went to Sunday school. AWANA, a church-sponsored club that focuses on teaching children Scripture, was an important part of their growing-up years. We believed in hiding God's Word deep in their hearts. I also read the Bible to them while they would eat breakfast, and Ken would have long conversations with them about godly attitudes and behavior.

When our oldest, Ryan, was in sixth grade, he was struggling academically. He had been in the local public elementary school up to this time. I felt like I would be sending him off a cliff if he continued on in a public middle school. I am sure he would have been labeled ADD—for Attention Deficit Disorder—if he had been tested. He was a typical boy who hated sitting in a chair for most of the day.

We decided I would homeschool him. This consisted of him reading for several hours a day and doing math. That was it! The rest of the school day was spent playing and eating. I would take Ryan, along with his cousin Gregory, to the beach to surf quite often. I had heard that a lot of physical activity was beneficial for good brain development in children, which is why he also participated in sports practices and games during the after-school hours.

I think it's terrible how young children, especially boys, are made to sit in hard chairs for hours every day. So much of that time is wasted in discipline problems, filling out boring handouts, and teachers teaching to the lowest common denominator.

Since Ryan was such a good reader, he did great when we put him in a Christian high school for his junior year. We found that if boys are good readers and good at math, all the other subjects come easily to them. Ryan went on to graduate from high school and go on to Biola University, where he graduated with a degree in Biology.

I also homeschooled our other son, Steven, from fifth grade to eighth grade. He never liked school and sitting for long, even though he did well academically. I did the same curriculum with him—a lot of reading and math. He went to a Christian high school for all four years and did great.

Steven also went to Biola for three years, left a year early to go to a three-year dental school, and then graduated from orthodontic school a few years after that. I believe only good things came out of homeschooling my children for a season in their lives. Best of all, they all are good readers who *love* to read now.

One mother wrote this about homeschooling on my blog:

> For our family, it's not necessarily trying to figure out what's wrong with public school. We focus on the benefits of homeschooling and that is enough to convince us.
>
> Bonding time with Mom, an opportunity to teach life skills as well as academics, equipping them to know/defend/love their faith and the Lord, bonding them as siblings, time to play and be

creative, clean house/healthy meals/simple living because Mom is home, control over influences, opportunities to serve outside of normal church times, ability to explore interests fully, and lack of busyness . . . the list goes on and on.

It's a simple life focused on loving the Lord and cherishing the years we have with our children when they're small.

Cassi, our youngest, wanted to go to the local middle school since she was lonely being at home all by herself. I told her she could go but that as soon as I felt that she was going in the wrong direction, I would pull her out. She lasted several months when I quickly saw that it wasn't a good match. Cassi was then homeschooled until ninth grade when she attended a Christian high school that she sailed through with fabulous grades.

I'm not sure the Lord wants us to send our children to a government-run school where they mandate that God not be mentioned, and where humanistic and evolutionary ideas are promoted. Also, this would allow a government institution to teach our children for the majority of their waking hours, even though the Bible clearly tells parents that they are to be the ones to train up their children in the way they should go in the nurture and admonition of the Lord. (See Deuteronomy 6:4-7.) To give this responsibility over to complete strangers who don't have God's instructions at heart seems wrong to me now. While I understand that homeschooling is not an option for everyone, a Christian education is paramount in importance.

If I had to do it all over again, I would homeschool our children from kindergarten on and then look into a Christian high school or one of the great homeschool programs available today since private schools can be expensive. I didn't know many people who homeschooled their children when my children were young, but I sure love how many Christian parents are homeschooling their children now. There's no way we can know what public school teachers are teaching our children or what they are exposed to by the other students.

Is this sheltering them? Yes, but they *should* be sheltered. I didn't want my children hanging out all day long with kids who used bad language and told dirty stories. No way did I want my children to go through what I went through: listening to teachers who taught lies and never taught about the Lord. God commands that we are to dwell upon the lovely and the good. He commands we walk with the wise, hate what is evil, and cling to what is good. He warns us that bad company corrupts good morals.

Children are not called to be missionaries to a lost world, but a lost world is exactly what they enter into when you send them to public schools. Christian adults in the public school system *are* missionaries, when you think about it, and need to be fully grounded in the Word of God. Yes, your children may be great witnesses at school by starting Bible studies and talking to others about the Lord, but years of exposure to the lies and filth they hear and see every day in the public school setting will take a toll on them. I have seen this happen to far too many children who were raised in godly homes. Public schooling is not worth our children's souls.

If your husband is against homeschooling, make an appeal to him as gently and respectfully as you can and then go about winning him without a word by being in subjection to him and exhibiting godly behavior. Pray the Lord will convict him and change his mind. Anything you see or hear about your children being exposed to—use that opportunity to tell him about it. Mention to him any bad behavior they are picking up, and let him know that if he changes his mind, you will do everything in your ability to be the best teacher to your children you can be.

We always spoke openly to our children about everything, including sex. Nothing was off limits. Yes, sometimes Ken and I embarrassed them, but we wanted them to learn everything from a biblical perspective and not a worldly perspective. We had high expectations for our children, yet they all knew they were loved and had a home to come home to every night—one where they felt loved and accepted.

Were we perfect parents? No! We failed at times, and all our children could tell you our faults, but they have also told us that we were great parents and they all love us very much. We are close to all four children and their families, and we all enjoy being together. It's only because of God's grace, mercy, and strength working mightily within us that we were able to accomplish anything good at all.

FROM A POST ON MY BLOG . . .

My greatest goal in raising children was to raise them in the nurture and the admonition of the Lord. Ken and I talked about the Lord to our children often. They knew exactly where we stood—on the Rock of our salvation.

Right after Steven's wedding, he handed us two letters: one from him and one from Emily, his bride. He's given me permission to share his letter here. I think you'll enjoy reading what he has to say. His words will give you hope that you *can* raise godly offspring, which God said is one of the purposes of marriage (Malachi 2:15). Here is Steven's letter:

> Dear Mom and Dad,
>
> Today's a day I thought would never come, yet here it is. The day I commit my life to the most amazing young woman I have ever known. Our prayers finally paid off.
>
> I'm writing this letter to you in an attempt to say thank you. I've realized in my twenty-seven years on this earth that very few families are as blessed as ours. Thank you for the amazing family you have raised and specifically for the way you have raised me. I know without a shadow of a doubt that I would not be where I am today without both of your guidance, leadership, and love.
>
> Mom, thank you for the countless hours you spent changing my diapers, making healthy meals for me, driving me to sports games and to school, home schooling me, praying for me, and loving me. Most importantly, thank you so much for the way you have shined the love of Jesus to me each and every day.
>
> I will never forget the many hours you spent teaching us about the Word of God and reading us the Bible in the morning. Lastly, thank you for being such an amazing example to me. The way you have endured so many years of pain and suffering, yet have never wavered in your faith, is

something I respect deeply about you.

It's easy to say the right thing every once in a while, but being with you at home on a daily basis, I know your faith has never faltered. You are a true woman of God, and my hope and prayer is that one day my children will be able to learn from their amazing grandma. I love you so much.

Dad, you have always been the rock of our family. If there is ever a need, you are the first to respond. Thank you for spending the time to build a relationship with me and teach me. Thank you for the countless hours you spent throwing at batting practice, hitting ground balls, shagging baseballs, helping with my homework, driving me all over California for games, filming my games, rebounding basketballs, teaching me how to shoot, throw, hit, and kick, and financially supporting me. I owe you big time and I hope that in the years to come, I can begin to start taking care of you for all you have done for me. Lastly, thank you for coming into my room at five years of age and sharing with me the love of Jesus and praying with me that I may accept Him into my life. Although that was a long time ago and I was very young, I will never forget you leading me in praying for my soul. From that moment, you never ceased teaching me about Jesus, and I thank you for this.

Finally, thank you both for the example you have set of a faithful marriage. I know you struggled in the first twenty-three years of your marriage, yet the way you both love one another now is something I truly admire. Thank you for this display of Christlike love, and for setting such an incredible example for Emily and me to follow.

> I love you so much,
> Steven

One young woman who I have been mentoring said, "Steven's letter was amazing. I shared it with my husband, and he thought so as well. We aspire to be godly parents for our children, but it has been hard for us to have a solid relationship with the Lord. It's been a struggle for many years."

Neither of them were raised in godly homes, and both have deep sin issues they struggle with.

"Don't worry," I replied. "You *will* get this! You both have the Lord of the Universe living inside of you, so never give up."

Yes, it is more difficult to raise children if you weren't taught the ways of the Lord growing up, but with God's power working mightily within you, you, too, can raise your children in the nurture and the admonition of the Lord.

10
Birth Control and Having Children

When God gave the command to be fruitful and multiply in Genesis 1:28, that wasn't just so the people of old could build up their population. In fact, His Word still stands today, and He has never changed this command. God tells us that children are a blessing and a gift; blessed is the man who has a quiver full of them.

God wants us to have children. The possibility of conceiving and bearing children can happen early and often in a loving marital relationship because men are almost always ready for sex. Women usually love sex when they are ovulating and their body is preparing to become pregnant. Birth control pills, however, have many side effects and can make women quite ill. Birth control pills stop a normal bodily function, which is the woman's monthly period, and some pills can even abort the egg if it's been fertilized.

The diaphragm, which requires you to also use a spermicide, comes with a warning saying that it can cause cancer (at least it did when I used it many years ago). Why would we want to put toxic chemicals inside of our bodies? The diaphragm is also uncomfortable, difficult to remove at times, and can also cause toxic shock syndrome if left inside the vagina too long.

I looked on the U.S. Department of Health and Human Services Women's Health website for an explanation of all forms of birth control and their side effects. I will list a few of them:

- **Sterilization.** For women, this is known as getting your tubes tied. There can be complications from the surgery and a risk of ectopic pregnancy, which involves the implantation of the fertilized egg outside of the uterus.

- **Vasectomy.** On the guy's side, complications may include bleeding under the skin and inflammation of the tubes that move sperm from the testicles.

- **Intrauterine device.** An IUD can cause irregular menstrual periods, pelvic inflammatory disease, back pain, nausea and vomiting, and infertility by tearing a hole in the uterus.

- **Birth control pills.** The side effects include high blood pressure, blood clots, heart attack, stroke, vision problems, and possible abortifacient.

- **Condoms.** The only side effect with a condom may be sensitivities, but in my opinion, they are not that much fun and take away the pleasure of sex.

- **Natural Family Planning (NFP).** This overlooked form of birth control relies on fertility awareness and knowing your monthly cycle. There are no side effects, except maybe having a precious baby.

I will repeat my original statement: *God wants us to have children.* Since certain birth control measures come with health risks and unwanted side effects, and some take the fun and spontaneity out of making love, does that mean I believe no one should use birth control and just wing it, like many families did in the past? No. Each couple must decide for themselves what to do about birth control, with the husband having the final say since he is the head of the wife.

If you want a lot of children but your husband does not, you must obey your husband. A woman who goes against her husband in this decision will suffer the consequences. A much better way to handle the question of children is to gently give your husband all the facts, your opinion, and then leave it in the Lord's hands. Trust your husband with what he decides.

After Cassi, our fourth child, was born, we used the rhythm method, meaning that intercourse was restricted to the times of my monthly cycle when ovulation was least likely to occur. Although the rhythm method worked as advertised, the big problem for me was that during the times when I used to enjoy lovemaking the most, we couldn't have sex! So this wasn't a great method for us in the end.

When we were in our early forties, Ken and I were convicted about having all the children God wanted us to have. We stopped using birth control, but unbeknown to us I had a brain tumor, which caused me to not be able to conceive. I would learn later on that the tumor was pushing against my pituitary gland, which is the organ that controls most of our hormones.

Outside of your marriage, you must not approach couples and tell them how many children they should have. It's none of your business. This serious and important matter is between the husband and wife, and the husband should have the final say.

Yes, I have described some of the side effects of different birth control methods, but our husbands will be the ones standing before the Lord to account for the decisions they made in their homes, not us. We will only have to give account for the way we lived our lives and our submission, or lack of it, to our husband's authority.

In conclusion, prayerfully discuss this important area of married life with your husband and respect his decision. It's much more important and clear in God's Word that wives are to submit to their husbands than it is to have all the children God wants you to have.

FROM A POST ON MY BLOG . . .

Her heart aches for children.

Andrea is doing everything she can to be a loving wife and appreciate her husband just the way he is, even though he's not ready for children yet.

When I mentioned Andrea's story to Erin, my

daughter-in-law, and described how this husband wants to have all his ducks in order . . . like getting established in his career, paying down student loan and credit card debt, buying a home, and having some money in a savings account, Erin responded, "He'd rather have ducks than babies!"

We shared a laugh, but I don't blame men who feel this way. They carry the burden of providing for a family. Society tells them that children are expensive and deserve the best education money can buy, but I go back to the Bible for direction.

When the Israelites were in bondage in Egypt (they were slaves), the way they grew to be so powerful was by having children—and God blessed them with a lot of children. But there's a bigger message being conveyed here, and it's that the Lord is our provider. I think men forget this important promise. The fear of having children too soon or having too many usually comes down to fear and not trusting God as our provider.

My mom was raised during the Great Depression. Her dad was a milkman. They had seven children. My mom said they were definitely poor compared to today's standards, but she never knew they were poor. All of their needs were met.

We live in the wealthiest nation the world has ever known and all of our needs (and wants) are abundantly provided for us, yet so many of us live in great fear. Where is faith and trust in God? He owns the cattle on a thousand hills!

Look at the way He created our bodies. Men are ready for sex almost all the time. Women enjoy sex the most when they are ovulating. Hmmm, do you think God wants us to have babies?

I realize some women shouldn't have any more children because of health problems. The whole issue of when and how many children to bring into this world comes down to what each husband and wife decides.

So if you have a husband who isn't ready to have children or doesn't want anymore, my advice to you is to give it completely over to the Lord and let Him work on your husband. Being upset or angry doesn't get you anywhere. Love him, serve him, please him, and pray for him.

God works powerfully in others. I've heard of many husbands changing their minds about having children and how many. You have a much better chance of changing his mind by continuing to be loving and gentle with him, instead of trying to manipulate him.

I do have a funny story with which to end this post. When Ken told me I could stay home full time after I had my second baby, I was a full-time schoolteacher. I wanted to be a stay-at-home mom so badly that I put a hole in my diaphragm and we conceived Ryan! I can't tell you how thrilled I was when I learned I could stay home and raise my babies.

Now, I don't recommend using deceit to get your way. I wasn't a submissive wife back then, but I did get to stay home. That said, nothing is worth harming the relationship between you and your husband. It would have been better for me to trust and believe in Him, for He alone is worthy.

11
The Dating Scene and Sexual Purity

When my oldest child, Alyssa, was nearing her Sweet Sixteen birthday, we heard a speaker at our Sunday school class talk about teaching your children not to date.

"Nothing good comes out of dating—only broken hearts and all too often, purity is lost," he said. "Dating also prepares children for a divorce type of mentality. When things aren't working out or you've lost feelings for each other or get angry, you call it quits. Easy in, easy out."

What this speaker said made a lot of sense to Ken and me, so we decided to encourage our children not to date during high school.

This didn't mean they couldn't go to the prom, but we asked that they go with another couple or a close friend. We didn't want them to be alone with a member of the opposite sex, especially if there were feelings going on between them. We were more lenient about this if they were going out just as friends.

Ken and I, however, didn't worry too much about the emotional purity that many espouse today since it seemed natural for teens to have "crushes" on members of the opposite sex and they had to learn to work through those feelings. We realized we couldn't protect them from everything. A couple of our children went through emotional heartbreaks during their teen years, but they quickly recovered.

Once our four children graduated from high school, we encouraged them to date with a purpose—and that purpose was to figure out if the person they were dating was marriage material. They all definitely wanted to marry someone who was deeply committed to the Lord. They also wanted someone who would be a good parent, desired to raise children, was fun to be around, and who they were attracted to.

All of us are called to sexual purity, and there are plenty of Bible verses concerning immorality. Here are two that stand out:

> *Flee immorality. Every other sin that a man commits is outside the body, but the immoral man sins against his own body.*
>
> 1 CORINTHIANS 6:18 (NASB)

> *For this is the will of God, your sanctification; that is, that you abstain from sexual immorality; that each of you know how to possess his own vessel in sanctification and honor, not in lustful passion, like the Gentiles who do not know God . . .*
>
> 1 THESSALONIANS 4:3-5 (NASB)

God wants us to be set apart and holy. He wants us to be lovers of Himself and not lovers of pleasure. He commands us to practice self-control and abstinence until marriage and keep the marriage bed undefiled. You must diligently teach these principles of righteous living to your children—or they won't hear it. Instead, the message they will hear from the world is this: "If it feels right, do it."

You must protect your sons—and your daughters, too, believe it or not—from pornography. Most admit to becoming addicted to pornography in middle school. This is why we home-schooled our boys through junior high. We gave them books like *Every Young Man's Battle* to read in order to prepare them for the temptations they would face in the world.

This is a battle that's been around a long time. I remember when I was in public junior high and was walking down the school hallway. That's when I spotted a picture of a naked woman on the floor. As I walked by, I noticed some boys watching me, smirking as they waited to see my reaction.

These days, boys don't have to cut out a centerfold and leave it on the ground—they can just point their iPhones at a girl and show her all sorts of pornography. I shudder thinking how easy it is for boys (and girls) to access porn through a wireless connection to one of their devices. But even if you're off the grid, pictures of naked and half-naked women are everywhere, from movies to TV shows to billboards to magazines.

This is why you must teach your young sons and daughters from an early age to flee sexual immorality—and that starts by making a covenant to not look at naked men and women. Tell them how destructive this can be and how it has the potential of ruining their future marriage since the "comparison game" can be easily played. For the boys, tell them what porn does to a man's brain—causing a surge in the chemical dopamine, the neurotransmitter responsible for feelings of pleasure. That's why men get addicted to porn, but repeated dopamine surges mean the brain can become desensitized to sex and dull the response to sexual stimulation.

Porn abuses women and treats them like sex objects instead of women with value. Tell them that looking at porn is like touching a hot stove, meaning they will end up getting burned. That's why I recommend reading several verses from Proverbs—especially Chapter 5—to your children every day and discussing what God is trying to teach them.

My older son, Ryan, thanked me recently for protecting him when he was growing up. He knows many men who are addicted to pornography. The Bible describes a prostitute—or one of today's porn stars—like this: "The lips of an adulteress drip honey, and smoother than oil is her speech; but in the end she is bitter as wormwood, sharp as a two-edged sword" (Proverbs 5:3-4, NASB).

This is every man's battle. This is a battle we must prepare our sons for and remind them that God is working mightily within them so they can be overcomers.

THE DATING SCENE

Let me return to the high school dating scene, which does not lend itself to purity. There is no good reason for two teenagers of the opposite sex—with raging hormones—to ever be alone. Everything should be done in groups and for the purpose of having fun, nothing else. When they are ready to marry, then they can begin searching for the right one.

Yes, I said searching. I don't think God just wants us to sit around and wait. Isaac went searching for his bride, and Ruth made herself available to Boaz. Many put great effort into preparing for a job through education, applying, and searching. The same effort should be made in finding a spouse. You want to help prepare your children to put energy and effort into finding the right person to marry.

I think it's fine for singles to use online dating services to help them find that special person. There are a bunch of excellent Christian ones—eHarmony, Christian Mingle, and Zoosk—and match.com has a big Christian section. I know several couples who found their spouses this way. Finding a good Bible-believing church and getting involved in the singles group is another great way to find your mate. Remind your children to look their best and be joyful because others are attracted to joyfulness. No one likes to be around a pessimistic person who complains.

When they meet someone they are interested in, get to know them. Ask them questions and let them become involved in your family. Two of my children's spouses lived with us for a few months before they married our children because that was the best situation for them. We got to know them very well, and they in turn got to know Ken and me.

Raise your children in the nurture and admonition of the Lord, work to have open communication with them, and if they are not rebellious, they should grow up to walk in the Truth. When they get older, they should look for a godly spouse, marry as a virgin, and begin a whole new generation for God's kingdom. It doesn't get better than that.

A parent must be diligent about protecting their children from sexual abuse. With sexual immorality and pornography rampant, you cannot just sit by and do nothing. Sex predators are abusing little girls and boys even in the bushes at the park! They do it when your children are out playing with their friends. It's really happening, and I hear about it way too often.

You must instruct your children from a young age so they will be well educated in what is proper behavior as a teenager and then as an adult. That way a child can recognize and respond to aberrant behavior. My mentor and colleague Debi Pearl has written two great books—*Samuel Learns to Yell and Tell* and *Sara Sue Learns to Yell and Tell*—that you need to read to your children so that they can be aware of the dangers around them.

You can also share with them one of my blog posts called *Take Porn by the Horn,* which was written by Michael Pearl. If you have sons, I would encourage you to have them read it.

We live in a dark and decaying society. Arm your children with God's Truth and be careful with whom your children are allowed to spend time. Pray for God's hedge of protection around them.

THE LIGHTER SIDE

When I was young, around ten or so, I was at my neighbor's home across the street. She told me her parents had sex a lot. I told her my parents were Christians and only had sex three times!

When my sons were young, one of them asked Ken if he had sex with me only four times since we had four children. Ken looked at them and asked, "Four times this week?"

After I explained to the TheJoyFilledWife how we taught our children about sex, she wrote me this about her childhood:

> How I wish I had been raised up with that kind of influence from my parents. Most of the time, my parents went to bed separately, slept with their door open, or had one of my younger siblings asleep in their bed between them.

I don't recall *ever* seeing my parents show affection, except for holidays when they would exchange a small peck after they opened their gifts from each other. That was hard on me growing up, especially with affection being so important to me. The truth is, my parents spent most of their time complaining to us about each other, and I remember wondering throughout my childhood if I was going to wake up one day to find out that my parents were divorcing. I longed to have a biblical, affectionate marriage one day and knew that I would need to go to Scripture for that example since my parents didn't model that.

I remember spending time with friends who would say how grossed out they were that they overheard their parents having sex. I never told them, but I would have gladly traded places with them, if for no other reason than to take comfort in knowing that my parents still desired each other.

TheJoyFilledWife told me that all of her siblings grew up to have warped views about sex. They either became sexually promiscuous or overly conservative, where they even viewed sexual affection in marriage as dirty. While some of her siblings think that doing "anything with anybody" is perfectly acceptable, others think that French-kissing your spouse or being in a sexual position outside of the traditional "missionary" style is worldly and disgusting.

So how do we teach children that sex between a married couple should be fun, especially in a society that views sex between a married couple as boring and unexciting? I mean, when is the last time a Hollywood movie featured a married couple having sex? Just about never . . . .

So let me tell you how we raised our children in this area. After the boys asked Ken about how many times we had sex, Ken sat both boys down and explained the facts of life in this area. We were always open with our children. They knew if our door was locked, they were not to disturb us. We didn't allow our children to ever sleep in our bed. We weren't afraid to hug and kiss in front of them. They knew we enjoyed sex and were raised to understand that making love inside the confines of marriage is a good thing, and that sex outside of marriage is against God's instructions and therefore a sin.

We told them they needed to wait until marriage to have sex and gave them understandable boundaries in order to help them attain these goals. We explained all the terrible consequences of sex outside of marriage—unplanned pregnancies, sexually transmitted diseases, and decreased marital stability—and touted the role of sex in marriage: enjoying each other's bodies and making precious babies.

Our children always knew that sex inside of marriage was never something dirty, but that it was a gift from God worth saving for their spouses. From the looks of things, all four of our children all appear to be *very* happily married. Actually, they have all told me they *love* being married!

> *Let your fountain be blessed, and rejoice in the wife of your youth. As a loving hind and a graceful doe, let her breasts satisfy you at all times; be exhilarated always with her love.*
>
> Proverbs 5:18-19 (NASB)

FROM A POST ON MY BLOG . . .

My daughter-in-law, Emily, was raised the way we raised our children. She never kissed a man until she kissed our son Steven at the age of twenty-four.

Before her wedding, I asked Emily if she would write about their love in a letter. With her permission, I'm sure you will enjoy her thoughts:

> As a little girl, when I realized that I could not marry my Daddy, whom I adored, I started to think about the kind of man I would marry someday.
>
> *He's got to be able to make pancakes,* I thought, *and he should be strong enough to throw kids in the air while in the pool.* These were the kind of manly things I knew were essential to a good husband. As I grew older, this list grew longer.
>
> After high school, I attended a fantastic Christian college—Wheaton College in the Chicago area—that some referred to as the "mecca of godly men." That's not why I attended Wheaton, but that was the reputation the college carried.
>
> Even though finding a husband wasn't the highest of my priorities during my undergrad-

uate education, I always thought in the back of my mind, *Well, if I can't find him here, where will I find him?*

Many of my friends found their spouses in college, and while I went on some dates, nothing ever panned out. I began to wonder when my time would come. Then I started to question if my standards were too high. I distinctly remember my mom sitting my younger sister and me down and reminding us not to look for someone just like our father because he was, indeed, not perfect. Mom was afraid that we idolized him so much that we held impossibly high standards for men our age.

I first heard about Steven Alexander through a mutual friend named Michal (a woman). We both attended Wheaton College, where she met the man she would marry, Brian Kolb, who had been one of Steven's best friends since childhood, having grown up together in the same hometown of Carlsbad.

When Michal found out I would be returning to my hometown of Houston after graduation, she immediately told me about a Biola University graduate named Steven Alexander who had recently moved to Houston to attend orthodontic school. Michal insisted that we should meet each other some day. I even have a text message from her that said something to the effect of *You just need to marry Steven so we can live next door to each other and our kids can be best friends and we can live happily ever after.*

If she only knew how right she would be! At the time, though, I didn't really think much of her text because friends had often tried to set me up in the past and nothing had ever panned out. Besides, even though Steven and I were in the same city, the chances of us ever meeting were still awfully remote.

After returning to Houston, I was swept up in the busyness of family, a new niece being born, going to law school, and finding a church. I started attending a wonderful church with my brother and sister-in-law and decided I wanted to call it my church home. Then a friend invited me to her adult singles Bible study after the Sunday evening service at this same church.

Since I was eager to make Christian friends, I readily accepted her invitation. I attended this Bible study two times and loved it, so I committed to becoming part of the singles adult group. On the third Sunday, as I was walking into church, I looked down at my phone and saw I had a missed call from a number with a California area code. Because I was already late for service and didn't recognize the number, I decided not to call back.

Following the service, during the Bible study, a handsome man stood before the class and asked for prayer for his mother's health as she was undergoing a serious operation. Little did I know this was my future husband speaking about my future mother-in-law!

After Bible study ended, this good-looking stranger came up to me and said, "Hi, are you Emily Rice? I'm Steven."

I'm sure I had a blank look on my face. Something wasn't registering. "Steven Alexander?" I guessed.

"Yeah, that's me. You're Michal's friend, right? I called you two hours ago."

Steven said that as he was driving to church that evening, he remembered that he had told Michal he would call her friend Emily, which he did.

"Didn't you get the voice mail?" he asked.

"No, I would have remembered that," I said.

Steven still claims that he left a voice mail, which I never received. At any rate, it was an amazing coincidence that we met. There were many, many churches in the Houston area, and the church where Steven and I met each other had over a dozen Bible studies for young single adults. Of all the churches and all the Bible studies I could have joined, I joined that one. God undoubtedly had a hand in us meeting.

I told my mom about the encounter when I got home. Although she didn't tell me this at the time, she thought, *Well, that would be a cool story to tell if they get married.*

Over the next couple of months, Steven and I chatted at church and various social events, and it was nice talking to him. He could see I was focused on getting my law degree.

In December, we went on a fun coffee date, but I was distracted with my final exams. Although my head was saying, *This is a great guy!* my heart had some catching up to do.

Steven went home for a few weeks over Christmas, and I caught up on rest after an intense final exams period. In the beginning of January, he asked me to go running with him. I was with my mom and my sister Carolyn when he asked, and my initial reaction was, *No way! I can't run with this guy. He is so in shape! I will make a fool of myself.* But Mom and my sister practically answered for me and convinced me that I would be dumb not to go with him.

Fortunately, Steven ran at my pace, and we were able to hold a conversation for the entire three-mile run. We went to dinner that evening and out for coffee after that. Five hours later, I arrived home feeling a little giddy. We had so much fun together. I had often said there are men I find attractive and intelligent, but I want to be with a man who can also make me laugh because I love to laugh! Well, Steven fit the bill, and the more I knew him, the more I wanted to know him.

Two weeks after that running date, we began "officially dating," you could say. He made his intentions known, and it was then that I truly felt I could let my guard down around him. You see, I've never been much of a flirt, and, looking back, I can see how I was hard to read in the beginning. But Steven says he loves that I was guarded because it showed him that I was that way around all guys.

On Valentine's Day, I shared one of my journal entries with Steven that I had written three days prior to our running date. I felt the Lord telling me to pray for my future husband, so I wrote, "Not sure why, but something tells me my time is coming soon." Little did I know how soon!

We dated three-and-a-half months prior to our engagement, which also lasted three-and-a-half months. The support from family and friends confirmed that Steven was the one and that our relationship was from God.

I used to see people getting married after six months and think, *They are crazy. There is no way they know each other well enough!* I couldn't have been more wrong.

Did I know every one of Steven's habits and mannerisms?

No. But a couple who has been dating two years wouldn't know every detail either.

Did I know his character?

Yes.

Did I know his commitment to family and love for the Lord?

Absolutely.

Did I trust in my Heavenly Father who has protected and provided for me my entire life, and who has placed such an amazing man in my life?

You bet.

There are no guarantees in this life apart from what God has promised in His Word. I believe God when He promises that good things will come to those who wait on Him. My good thing happened to be a tall, dark, and handsome surfer who was sold out for Jesus.

I'll end with one of my favorite quotes by Charles Stanley: "Our willingness to wait reveals the value we place on the object we are waiting for."

The Lord has protected me my entire life, and especially during my time of dating. Looking back, I see nothing but evidence of God's grace in my life, and I recognize that I can take no credit for His work.

To young single women out there: keep fighting the good fight. I've been there, and I know the feeling of longing for intimacy and marriage. It's funny because I'm a week away from my wedding, marrying the man of my dreams.

While I am happier than I've ever been, I've realize, still, that nothing can compare to the love of our Savior Jesus Christ. I won't tell you that your Prince Charming is on his way because I don't know what God has planned for you. But I do know the Truth that the Lord will never abandon you or forsake you. His promises are good, and He desires the greatest intimacy you will ever experience. Abide in Him, and see that He is good.

While the wedding is exciting and I can't wait to see all our friends and family together, it's the marriage I am most excited about. I said recently that even though Steven is a dream come true for the twenty-five-year-old me, this was also my dream when I was thirteen years old.

In case you're wondering, Steven is definitely strong enough to throw kids in the pool, and though the jury is still out on the pancakes, who knows . . . maybe this story will encourage some creativity in the kitchen!

12
Keepers at Home

*E*ncouraging women to be keepers at home is the most controversial topic on my blog, bar none. It seems like a lot of women *want* to work outside of the home, which surprises me, so they give me an earful whenever I write about the positive side of being a stay-at-home mom.

Staying home full time is difficult, I admit, but working outside of the home on top of raising children, keeping a home clean and tidy, being a help meet to your husband, and fixing nourishing food is usually too much for anyone. Something will get neglected, and it's usually the husband, who should be our first priority.

I take seriously the command that young women are to be keepers at home and guide family life under the same roof. The life of the Proverbs 31 woman revolved around the home. She fed her family, made their clothes, managed the servants, bought a field and planted a garden, sewed clothes to sell for a little extra income, and must have taken good care of her husband since he rose up and called her blessed.

Studies have proven that children need their mothers. If children don't have their mothers to bond with full time when they are babies and toddlers, they will have a much more difficult time bonding to others as they grow up. They will be more prone to depression, insecurity, and emotional instability as adults, according to various studies, including one from the *Journal of Clinical Child and Adolescent Psychology*.

When mothers are home full time, the children feel secure that someone is always there for them. When they are sick, she is there. When they come home from school and need to talk with someone, she is there. When she feeds them, reads to them, hugs them, and cares for their needs, they feel loved. As they get older, she needs to be home to protect them from watching inappropriate TV shows and going online to look at pornography. She plays a vital role in helping them navigate through the difficult and emotionally turbulent teenage years.

Parents are given the command to teach their children the ways of God. The bulk of the training and discipline falls on the mother's shoulders because she is around the children all day—or should be. No one can take the place of a mother at home. She is the heart of the home and that is where her heart should be. When she realizes her value in running the household and understands that meeting the needs of her husband and children is a ministry from the Lord, she will be content caring for her family and being a living sacrifice for them.

I worked as a full-time schoolteacher for the first two years of Alyssa's life (my oldest child), which I will regret doing until the day I die. Life was exhausting, and I felt guilty all the time for leaving her with either my mother, a young woman at a day-care facility, or with a neighbor. I remember sitting around the lunch table one day with a bunch of schoolteachers, and they all said if they had to do it all over again, they would not have children because their sons and daughters gave them so much heartache. They also said they were too tired when they got home to properly discipline, train, or comfort their children. These teachers didn't take pleasure in child-raising since their offspring were rebellious and not enjoyable to be around.

It takes a lot of time to train and teach children. You must continually be correcting bad behavior, disciplining disobedience, and replacing rambunctiousness with obedience, good manners, and healthy habits. You must train them to work hard, tell the truth, be kind, serve others, and most importantly, learn from God's Word. If you don't do the training, no one else will take the time to instruct your children in all these vitally important matters.

Women ask me if I think a mother working part time is okay. No, I don't think that's good either. I know that I didn't want to work part time when I had kids. I wanted to be with my children full time and they wanted this as well. Just ask those who work at day-care centers about the attitudes that children have after being left by their mothers. When I was a substitute teacher at a Christian school for a short time when my children were older, a schoolteacher shared with me that she could always tell which children had full-time mothers because they were much more secure and happy than those who didn't. Mothers being home full time creates security in their children.

If you are blessed to be home full time with your children, use your time wisely. Watching soap operas, allowing your home to become a pigsty, and letting the children run amok is not the way to go.

Remember, God is a God of beauty and order. Learn how to keep a clean and tidy home, not wasting time in front of the television or on the computer.

Watch your children consistently. Know who their friends

are and what they are doing at all times. Don't let them play with friends in their bedrooms, especially with the doors closed. Have them play out in an open room like a family room or somewhere off the kitchen so that they are within earshot of you and you can monitor what is being said. Take them outside a lot to play. Large motor movements are crucial to raising healthy, smart children. Going on walks or hikes together and getting them used to exercising will help them grow up to be strong and in shape.

Studying Proverbs 31 is a great exercise in learning all about being a keeper at home. When you read this last chapter in Proverbs, you'll notice that she had servants. No matter what your income level is, we have servants today as well: washing machines, dryers, dishwashers, stoves, microwave ovens, blenders, toasters, vacuum cleaners, lawn mowers, and many other things that make our lives much easier than when our ancestors lived.

Spend more time at home than you do anywhere else. Keep your home clean and organized by getting rid of clutter and only buying things you need. Live on your husband's income—whatever that may be—and be content. Live frugally if you have to and learn how to cook fresh, healthy food from scratch. Make your home a sanctuary that your family loves to spend time in, where there are mouth-watering aromas of home-cooked food and lots of laughter.

I encourage women, when they have young children, not to get too involved in activities outside of the home. You don't have to go to a ton of Bible studies, teach Sunday school, or be heavily involved in outside activities if that means you're neglecting your household responsibilities or family.

I'm an empty nester now, but I find if I'm away from home too often, I get behind in my housework. Your home and your family need to be your first priority. God has always honored the home, and the home is where women are most protected, comfortable, and have the greatest ministry by raising godly offspring. Even to women who are barren, God's Word says, "He makes the barren woman to keep house, and to be a joyful mother of children" (Psalm 113:9, NASB).

MAKE YOUR HOME A MAGNET

One of the ways a keeper at home may be the biggest blessing to her neighbors, church, and community is through hospitality. Invite people over for dinner often, and if you have a guest room, make it ready to house someone in need on a moment's notice. Make your home a welcoming place for your children's friends to come by making fun snacks and inventing creative games for children to play. My home was always warm and inviting because Mom was almost always there for us. She loved having people over to feed them her home-cooked meals. All my friends wanted to be in my home.

Never let anyone make you feel guilty for being "only" a wife and mother. You should take joy in your role and be content in the ministry the Lord has given you. Even when all your children are grown and gone, your greatest ministry can still be in your home as you continue to serve your husband and do all of the shopping, cooking, and cleaning.

As you reach the middle-age years, you can spend your time teaching young women, as the Lord commands, and helping those in need. One of my sisters, Alisa, is using her empty-nest years to teach women about the importance of keeping their immune systems strong by eating healthy organic food, the way God created it.

Young women are desperate to be taught Truth, and they can hear about God's wisdom from women in a different season of life. This Scripture encapsulates it all:

> *Older women likewise are to be reverent in their behavior, not malicious gossips nor enslaved to much wine, teaching what is good so that they may encourage the young women to love their husbands, to love their children, to be sensible, pure, workers at home, kind, being subject to their own husbands, so that the word of God will not be dishonored.*
>
> Titus 2:3-5 (NASB)

I really like how the King James Version translates Titus 2:4-5, directing the younger women to be "sober, to love their husbands, to love their children, to be discreet, chaste, keepers at home, good, obedient to their own husbands, that the word of God be not blasphemed." Scripture seems clear to me here.

Once your children are grown and out of the house, use your time wisely by investing in the lives of young women, volunteering at church, babysitting your grandchildren—the list could go on and on. God wants us older women to teach younger women in His ways. If more older women had taken this role of mentor seriously, I believe that our churches and communities would be filled with women who joyfully serve their families from their homes, rather than looking much like the rest of the world with broken homes and broken families. All of our lives should be used in ministry to others.

The problem, as I see it, is that there are few older women out there available to mentor young women—and those that are available have no clue how to mentor them. Most of them don't know what submission to a husband looks like or what a keeper at home means. Many of them don't have good marriages and haven't taught their daughters how to cook or be housekeepers. The old joke about how the only thing a young wife knows how to make is reservations has a ring of truth to it.

The church has dropped the ball in this area. There are some pastors who preach about the importance of older women mentoring younger women, such as John MacArthur, Michael Pearl, and Voddie Baucham, but this message is not getting out there the way it should be, which is why I see this as part of my role as a blogger. I remember when Dr. James Dobson said on the *Focus on the Family* radio show years ago that mothers *need* to be home when the children are young. I also loved hearing Dr. Dobson remind listeners that when his two children grew up to become teenagers, he thought those years were the *most* important time for mothers to be at home.

"The heavy demands of child-rearing do not slacken with the passage of time," he said. "In reality, the teen years generate as much pressure on the parents as any other era."

In conclusion, young women, if you have children and if it is at all possible, I encourage you to be a full-time keeper at home. Take good care of your husband, the children God has blessed you with, and the home that you're living in. If your husband wants you to keep working outside the home, gently show him Scriptures concerning a mother being at home, and then pray fervently for the Lord to change his heart. Then become the best help meet possible and the best mother you can be and "win him without a word" as he observes your godly behavior. The power of a Transformed Wife is a powerful testimony and influence on others, as well as the most powerful one at our disposal. I hope you will choose to use it for God's glory.

Sure, you'll have to live within your husband's income, but God will be faithful to provide. If you're still working outside the home, show your husband the amount you really make after taxes are taken out, as well as the amounts you spend on day care, fast food, gas fill-ups, and any other expenses you incur since you aren't home full time (like wardrobe and car maintenance).

By the time you add up all your out-of-pocket expenses, as well as the cost of transportation and day care, you're usually only netting a few bucks an hour—money that can be saved just by you cooking a home-cooked meal each night! And don't forget that children much prefer their mothers at home to having more stuff.

So hearken to hearth and home, my friend. No woman, at the end of her life, will regret that she was there for her children when it mattered most.

FROM A READER OF MY BLOG . . .

I'm ending this chapter with a comment from one of my readers named HisHelper about mothers being keepers at home:

> Maybe we need to take a look at not only the letter of the law—meaning the specific, literal, physical actions and directives of what the law demands— but also the spirit of the law—fulfilling the intent of the law, which involves not only our physical

bodies doing something but also the content of our hearts.

Please pay careful attention to these definitions as I am not using these terms to water down the letter of the law in order to make way for the flood of "what ifs" and exceptions that can easily put our focus on to the exclusion of all else. What I'm saying is that every scriptural example we have of a person coming to Jesus and telling him that he had fulfilled the law or had "checked the boxes" discovered there was something even more required!

As a wife and mother, I could lock myself in my house twenty-four hours a day and never leave and be able to say with a truthful face that I am a keeper at home, all the while being completely absent mentally and emotionally from my family. The dishes might get done and the floors mopped, but even if I'm physically there, I can be absent. In these situations, the box is checked, the letter of the law is fulfilled, but we all know that is not the intent or the spirit of the law.

So, what is the spirit of the law in this case? What higher purpose is the Lord calling us to?

Lori and others have written much about the purpose that is being fulfilled when we are keepers at home. I will summarize by saying that there is something incredibly powerful happening in our homes when not only our bodies are residing there, but also our hearts.

When we are looking well to the ways of our own household, we are not only enabling our husband to go out and provide—to slay dragons and to do what God has called him to do—but we, ladies, take on the powerful mantle of changing the world by shaping and molding generations for the Lord in a way that no one else can.

We are able to carry out the mandate to disciple our children—in our homes, when we walk along the way, when we rise up, and when we lie down (Deuteronomy 11:19). So, yes, we may be seen out and about, but look who is right beside us—our little ones. Where are our hearts? Right there with our families.

Truth be told, this is not always convenient or without extra work. Training and disciplining children is hard work and requires diligence and perseverance. Repetitive tasks can be monotonous at times, and there is often little appreciation shown for those tasks that go unnoticed by all—except for our Father! If you are missing the mark of your calling, the very thing you were created to be as a wife, how could you truly be fulfilled?

Should we not aspire to something greater than checking the box, such as greatness in our calling? Going beyond what is "required" and walking the extra mile? Striving to be the biggest blessing to our husbands and families?

Because of this, I believe that our actions and decisions we make should spring forth from a desire to fulfill not only the letter of the law, but also the intent of the law and the spirit of the law. Of course, we cannot do this in our own power, but by His Spirit. Sure, we will at times stumble and fall short. Thank the Lord for His grace and mercy that covers us and allows us to get back up and start again.

When it comes down to it, each family will look different in how this is carried out. Maybe a young mom is fortunate to have loving grandparents living nearby. Maybe she has the opportunity for the children to go to Grandma's house for a few hours a week so she can pursue an outside interest. Maybe the whole family travels with Dad for several days each month. Mom is obviously not anywhere near her house, but the intent of the law is being fulfilled: her heart is with her family. She is physically, emotionally, mentally, and spiritually available, caring for her household.

I just want to challenge each of us, including myself, by asking this question: *Where is your heart?*

I pray we can answer this question by saying that, first and foremost, we have our hearts set on Jesus, walking in grace and in the joy of our salvation, and desiring to be obedient to His commands for the purpose of His glory.

When we truly understand God's wise and loving plan, and choose to obey it without fear, I believe we will naturally find our hearts turning toward our husbands and children.

Renew your mind in the truth of His Word, for He is trustworthy in what He has established. He has not left us in the dark about His beautiful, practical, and generationally minded plan for wives.

Not only does He so intimately know us, but He has fearfully created and wonderfully equipped us for such a calling as this.

13
How Are You Dressing?

As believers in Jesus Christ who want to please Him in every area of our life, modesty should be something we take a deep interest in since the Lord has called us to be modest. Anything that is important to Him should be important to us as well.

Some in the Church believe that women should only wear dresses, while others believe that any clothing type is appropriate, as long as it covers up a certain amount of skin or is not too tight or revealing. But is there a specific mandate for all women to follow? Many hold their convictions from this verse:

> *"A woman shall not wear man's clothing,*
> *nor shall a man put on a woman's clothing;*
> *for whoever does these things is an*
> *abomination to the Lord your God."*
>
> DEUTERONOMY 22:5 (NASB)

This verse is from the Mosaic Law, which we are no longer obliged to follow or live under. So, as Christians who live under the New Covenant, we have liberty to find out from godly older women, and especially our husbands, what modesty should look like for us.

Women should dress like women and be feminine, and men should dress like men and look masculine. The differences between the sexes should be easily and clearly discernible. Men should never wear women's clothing and vice versa. Even though we are no longer under the Law, we can learn from the Law about what God's heart is for His children. I follow the intent of this verse and have chosen to wear clothing that is noticeably different than what Ken wears. He would never want to wear my clothing, and I would never want to wear his.

More important to this discussion is 1 Timothy 2:9, which teaches that we are to adorn ourselves in "modesty," which I believe means we're not to dress in an alluring and seductive manner. In other words, we should avoid sheer and clingy material, plunging necklines, short shorts, skimpy dresses, and so forth. We shouldn't wear low-cut tops or dresses that expose half our breasts or offer guys a clear view. Modesty is an act of obedience to the Lord and an act of kindness to men by helping them to reign in their natural impulse to take long looks—which can lead to inappropriate thoughts.

And while I'm on the subject, the other big fashion statement for many women today is wearing yoga pants—the form-fitting fitness apparel that seems to be everywhere, from grocery stores to, well, even women's Bible studies. While comfortable as well as practical, tight-fitting yoga pants shape the derrière in ways that are like a push-up bra for your bottom. Skin tight in every way, I can assure you that yoga pants push the imagination buttons of most men everywhere and, like other immodest clothing, can trigger lustful thoughts.

Since lusting is a sin, woman are obligated to dress

in a manner that doesn't provoke lustful thoughts in a man. We must endeavor to not become obstacles that cause another person to sin in any area of their lives. Because men are easily stimulated visually, and woman are the objects of that stimulation, we must seriously take the responsibility of modest appearance. Women shouldn't be a stumbling block in a man's life on his road to purity.

Any honest man will tell you that lusting happens anytime he sees something that starts his motor running. I believe anything we women can do to help the guys *not* to lust is the way God wants us to dress. Wearing yoga pants creates a strong attraction for a man to look at a woman's body in a way that triggers lustful thoughts. It's hard for guys not to look for as long as they can. That's the way they are wired.

Since lusting is a sin, we ladies need to help them out by not becoming an obstacle that stands between them and the purity of mind God calls them to. As Jesus said in Matthew 5:28 (NASB), "But I say to you that everyone who looks at a woman with lust for her has already committed adultery with her in his heart."

Back in the '80s, I wore black leggings when they first came into style, but then Ken asked me not to wear them unless I wore a long shirt over them, citing the reasons I've just explained. I had no problem tossing my black leggings into the closet back then and have no problem not being part of the yoga pants crowd today. Every woman has to decide—with the help of the man in her life and others who will be honest with her—what constitutes modesty. I strongly believe that we should dress as women of God and do nothing that causes our brothers in the Lord to trip up or sin against the Word of God.

If you look around at today's culture, where many women dress in ways that leave little to the imagination, it's easy to say that these women have either no idea what they're doing or they have no reservations. Keep in mind these words from Jesus: "Woe to the world because of its stumbling blocks! For it is inevitable that stumbling blocks come; but woe to that man through whom the stumbling block comes!" (Matthew 18:7, NASB)

"That man" also refers to women, and when women dress immodestly and indecently, they are stumbling blocks. You never want to incur the Lord's wrath or hear Him say "woe" to you. While obviously not good, it is at least understandable when non-Christian woman dress provocatively. They are following the norms of our society that teaches and promotes promiscuous behavior. But women of God let our choices in dress proclaim a different message, one that honors God and takes into account our responsibility to our brothers in Christ.

Swimwear deserves its own mention as a category of apparel. Let me be clear: a bikini is not modest. I'm sorry, but it's not. Merely covering up your private parts doesn't qualify as being chaste. Ask any man, and he'll quickly tell you that the more flesh a woman shows, the more difficult it is for him to keep his thoughts under control.

When I go to the beach here in Southern California, I like to wear board shorts with a tankini top. That works for me and keeps me modest. Whenever I teach on this touchy subject, I've heard some women retort, "Some men will lust if a woman is wearing a garbage bag. It's *their* problem!"

Regardless, you are responsible to do everything in your power to not cause men to lust. The majority of men will not lust after women wearing garbage bags. They lust when a woman shows a lot of flesh or tightly fitted clothes.

When God directed us to dress modestly, He did that not only for our protection but for the men around us.

FROM A POST ON MY BLOG . . .

Every Saturday morning, Ken and I walk along the beach and eat at our favorite breakfast place with my parents. Then, on our walk back, Ken runs and walks up and down a long, steep set of stairs to the parking lot five or more times. He loves the exercise, and we enjoy this special time together. It's also my parents' highlight of the week.

Recently, we took our grandchildren with us and while Ken was running up and down, the grandchildren and I played in the sand near the bottom of the stairs. After a short while, Ken came over to me and told me we should leave because the view had changed.

"You'll see what I mean if you look around," he said.

I stood up to leave and was gathering the grandchildren when I turned around. Nearby, at the bottom of the stairs, a young woman was laying on her towel on her stomach. She was wearing a bikini with a stretch thong bottom that showed her entire buttocks—a view, I'm sure, that caught the eye of the many male surfers walking down the stairs with surfboards under one arm.

Seeing her prompted me to recall a bit earlier during our walk when we passed six young women lying on their stomachs with their heads together in a circle. Each was wearing a thong bottom, so their entire rear ends were showing.

I'm thinking that it won't be long before they go topless. That's where this culture is heading since modesty is sneered at and thought to be old-fashioned. Do these attractive young women know that they aren't only causing teenagers and young men to lust, but older men and even grandfathers as well?

Turning men on has to be an ego thing for them. They like showing off their sexy bodies because they feel pride knowing men are looking at them. I hate to break the news to these young women, but the boys and men aren't looking at them with love or respect but as objects with which to satisfy their worldly lust. They don't care about their souls, what they're worth, or who they are. The only thing these men have on their minds is what they would like to do sexually with them.

The half-nude women on the beach showed no discretion. I'm going to go strong here and say they were practically naked and unashamed when they were only supposed to show their bodies like this to their husbands. I understand that many, if not all, of these women weren't married, but they are only thinking about themselves and seemed to enjoy turning other women's husbands on. In fact, the Bible says they are like pigs with a gold ring in their noses. As you can see, the Lord doesn't think too highly of their behavior.

Lindsay Harold, a woman who comments on my blog once in a while, weighed in with this observation:

> The desire to be desired in women is part of God's design for women's sexuality, but it has to be channeled in the right direction. A woman is supposed to be desired by her husband, to make him want her, and to revel in his appreciation of her body. But it is not right or appropriate for a woman to

desire or get this kind of attention from men who are not her husband.

We, as Christian women, must do much better and teach our daughters to be modest. We must teach them about a man's sexual drive and that they are visual in nature. We want a man to respect us for our inward beauty of a meek and quiet spirit, not for the amount of flesh we show.

Our clothing should never cause a man to stumble since we respect our brothers in Christ too much to do this to them. Never be responsible for causing someone else to stumble into sin. These women will be held just as accountable for their actions as the men who stumble.

Yes, men are commanded to flee sexual immorality, and this is why Ken informed us that we were taking off from the beach that day. It's too bad that this young woman didn't know she was causing great disappointment to our grandchildren when we had to pack up and leave due to her indiscretion.

* *

As a ring of gold in a swine's snout,
so is a beautiful woman who lacks discretion.
PROVERBS 11:22 (NASB)

14
Talking About Your Financial Health

When it comes to everyday "kitchen table" finances, one of the most difficult things for young families—or any family, for that matter—is to not go into debt.

I'm referring to consumer debt such as unpaid balances on credit cards and home equity lines of credit. This can cause a family to rely on payday loans or use pawn shops as a means to get money before the next paycheck arrives. Using credit cards, home equity lines of credit, payday loans, or pawn shops as a source of income is foolish and unsustainable. The high interest rates associated with these loans are a form of bondage.

The reason so many people are in deep debt is because many of them live right on the financial edge. Additionally, most people do not distinguish between "wants" and "needs." In actuality, we have very few "needs" and a tremendous amount of "wants." We spend and spend on "wants" while fooling ourselves that they are really "needs." Learn to differentiate between the two, and you will be better able to make wise purchasing decisions.

Perhaps you've heard that more than 60 percent of Americans have less than $1,000 in their savings accounts. I would imagine that many young families don't have enough money saved for a major car repair. If you're in this situation, please know that Ken and I have been there. We've had our moments of financial struggles, and there were times when we squirreled away a little money . . . and bam! The water heater broke, or the property tax was due.

But that's alright because we knew that God was and is in control. I would imagine you feel the same way, but it's hard to feel chipper when life is a financial scramble. It's my belief that today's American families—overtaxed and squeezed by stagnant pay—are barely keeping their noses above water. Many are living paycheck to paycheck and bracing themselves for the next financial calamity—like a leaky roof or unexpected hospitalization. And who knows where the money is coming from to pay for the next car, college bills, and looming retirement.

The pressure to live within your means places tremendous stresses on everyone, but if you can spend wisely on basic household expenses such as food, clothing, housing, transportation, and incidentals, you will realize significant savings, perhaps several hundred dollars or thousands of dollars each month. This can be the difference between families staying financially solvent or sinking further into debt.

Better yet, I think the Transformed Wife can be part of the solution instead of part of the problem. A stay-at-home mom can save a family all kinds of money, starting with having time to shop for the best deals on clothes, shoes, and groceries. She saves money by doing the house cleaning (no need to hire a maid service), as well as cooking and preparing healthy, delicious meals that are a fraction of what it costs to eat out. I've told young moms to look at the kitchen as a profit center.

I know that many of the moms I've mentored have confided that they are struggling to keep their heads above the water line, which places tremendous stress on their marriages and even causes fights. Thank goodness we enjoy a priceless advantage being God's children, meaning you can go to our Lord with financial concerns. He knows your financial situation, your stresses, and your needs.

Whenever you have an important buying decision, pray about it. Just as God can direct you to a dependable used car that won't break down every other month, He can also help you find a much-needed used pair of kids' soccer shoes at a garage sale.

NO NEED TO WORRY

In one of the most comforting passages of Scripture, Jesus says:

> *"For this reason I say to you, do not be worried about your life, as to what you will eat or what you will drink; nor for your body, as to what you will put on. Is not life more than food, and the body more than clothing? Look at the birds of the air, that they do not sow, nor reap nor gather into barns, and yet your heavenly Father feeds them. Are you not worth much more than they?"*
>
> MATTHEW 6:25-26 (NASB)

Although the Lord instructs us not to worry, it's human nature to be concerned about making it to the end of the month without dipping into a dwindling savings account.

Our consumerist society encourages us to overspend and to believe that more is always better. Blitzed with "Huge Sale!" advertisements everywhere we turn, you must be on guard against the formidable pressure to "get a good deal."

You face an extraordinary number of choices for where you can spend your money. Seventy-five years ago, your great-grandparents grew up in towns with one market, one hardware store, and one gas station. That changed rapidly in the 1950s, and these days, massive "supercenters," modern supermarkets, expansive warehouse clubs, and niche grocery stores have sprung up in the suburbs like mushrooms.

Your great-grandparents shopped at a local five-and-dime store; we can choose from Walmart, Target, and Kmart. They had one clothing store; you have Marshalls, Ross, T.J. Maxx, and Kohl's. They had seasonal sales; you have digital coupons from Michael's and Bed, Bath & Beyond flooding your smartphone. They had a Sears catalog book; you have instantaneous online shopping available 24/7. They had mail-order companies; you have Amazon with Sunday delivery possible. They paid with cash; you likely carry multiple credit cards.

Stay-at-home moms can make a big difference when it comes to the family budget because you have more time to hunt down bargains that can save your family plenty of money each month. Knowing this may help justify your decision to stay at home with your children.

DEALING WITH DEBT

Here's a fast and simple rule that may not be easy to do but is well worth considering: you should live within your means and only buy what you can afford.

I was raised to always live below what I earned, which

enables one to contribute to a savings account. Ken and I have always lived this way. Except for our homes, we buy everything with cash instead of borrowing money because of this advice from Scripture: "The rich rules over the poor, and the borrower becomes the lender's slave" (Proverbs 22:7, NASB). If we can help it, and we usually can, we don't want to be a slave to anyone.

Unfortunately, our society encourages borrowing and "installment debt" through the easy availability of credit cards. If at all possible, pay off your credit card balances and become debt-free. It may mean forgoing a family trip or tightening up the shopping budget for the next year or two, but I would suggest you pay your outstanding balance off as soon as you can. Becoming debt-free is a biblically-based important goal. You don't want to be slaves to anything or anyone.

I like living a frugal life, and I guess that you would as well. This doesn't mean you have to be a tightwad and cut up old shower curtains and turn them into baby bibs or collect clothes dryer lint to make stuffed animals for the kids. But you can produce your own cleaning supplies and laundry detergent, shop garage sales and thrift stores for used clothing, and peruse Craigslist for used bikes or appliances. Implement these ideas and you will see that for a fraction of the cost of new, you will have what you need. Unless there's an impressive sale going on, avoid the mall and outlet stores since "shopping" will only increase your "wants" and lead to dissatisfaction.

Another tactic to save money is to stop purchasing convenience foods. When you buy premade salads, ready-made lunches, and frozen entrées, the extra cost is significant because you're paying for the labor of the food preparation in addition to the cost of the food itself. Making meals from scratch is not only *way* healthier for you and your growing family, but it's much cheaper than having a pizza delivered to your front door. Visit your local farmer's market, where you can find unbelievable deals on in-season produce, with much of it organic and not sprayed with toxic pesticides. Build meals around vibrant salads and your favorite protein source like chicken, fish, or beef.

By saving a few dollars here and there on meal preparations and everyday family purchases, you'll be better able to live within a budget. But there's another aspect to keep in mind: saving money on household items may allow you to support that missionary family you met on furlough, or let you financially respond when your church announces a building drive. The Lord delights in our gifts—not because He needs them—but because we are faithful in supporting His work.

It's good stewardship to spend money wisely and stretch your husband's paycheck as far as you can if he is the only breadwinner in the family. The key word is *balance*. God has given us financial resources—be they limited or plentiful—and we are to be content in whatever our circumstances may be (Philippians 4:11, NASB).

CREDIT CARD DEBT

Nearly two hundred years ago, Charles Dickens wrote this in his book *David Copperfield*:

> *Annual income: twenty pounds*
> *Annual expenditure: 19.6 pounds*
> *Result: happiness*
> *Annual income: twenty pounds*
> *Annual expenditure: 20.6 pounds*
> *Result: misery*

What a concise reminder that spending less money than your income results in happiness, but spending more than you take in equals misery. Spending money that you don't have in your purse or checking account generally happens these days through credit cards.

The mindset of many Americans goes like this:

> I see that number on my monthly credit card bill. That's the total balance I owe, but I don't have to pay that amount. I only have to pay the minimum amount, which is conveniently printed in a box right next to the total balance figure. The minimum balance is a trifling amount. I can handle that.

I can't believe how many people think that a credit card doesn't have to be paid in full each and every month! They cavalierly make minimum payments every thirty days as they continue spending away, heaping each additional purchase onto their growing mountain of debt. Every day they prove Christian financial counselor Ron Blue right, who states that people who make a purchase with their credit card have a tendency to spend 34 percent more than they would have otherwise. Human nature being what it is, paying by cash or by personal check—and actually having to count out the money or handwrite the big numbers—acts as a governor on spending.

What people don't realize is that when you pay the minimum payment amount and spread the payments out over the maximum allowable time, you end up paying *way more* for that item. For instance, if you purchase a $350 Apple watch with an interest rate of 12 percent (which is low) and make the minimum payment of $15 a month, then the actual cost of the watch will be $400.55

when you finally pay it off twenty-seven months later. If you purchase that same Apple watch and your interest payment is 21 percent (which is the average rate these days), that $350 dollar watch will cost you $453.79 by the time you pay it off thirty months later at $15 per month. Of course, many families are not trying to pay off a $350 Apple watch.

Based on an analysis of Federal Reserve Statistics and other governmental data, the average household owes an astonishing $15,762 on their credit cards. These families are adding (and paying) at least $3,310 a year in interest (at 21 percent), which is a huge burden. Since American families have historically added 5 percent per year to this staggering amount, this figure will surely hurdle past the $20,000 mark—which means even more bondage.

It's obvious that most people never consider the real cost of buying now and paying later. Nor do they contemplate what Dave Ramsey, author of *The Total Money Makeover,* said about buying stuff on credit: "Too many times we buy things we don't need with money we don't have to impress people we don't like."

A massive amount of credit card debt is like reliving *Groundhog Day*: you're paying over and over for books you've already read, dinners you've already eaten, vacations you've already taken—and Apple watches that are outdated. Out-of-control credit card debt is stealing from your future to pay for the present, and that's a terrible way to go through life. Many people call it mortgaging your future.

Excuse my bluntness, but if you're still not seeing the light, then do the math—please. Who in their right mind would pay an extra 21 percent every time they made a purchase with a credit card? That's what it will cost you if you don't pay back the full amount within a year's time. Some people with low credit scores must pay usury rates of up to 29 percent.

Even if you shift balances to "low cost" cards, all you're doing is delaying the day of reckoning when your finances come tumbling down like a house of cards. In the game of credit cards—you versus the issuing bank—the house always wins. It's funny and somewhat sad that some folks will shop all around town to save $100 on a new refrigerator but never understand the futility of that effort when a new $2,500 charge is kneaded into the dough of their outstanding credit card balance.

There are other mechanisms that the credit card issuers employ to receive more of your hard-earned dollars. Did you know that the moment you charge a $2,500 refrigerator at your local big box store that you immediately start paying interest if you haven't paid off all outstanding balances? You don't receive a grace period when you're carrying unpaid balances forward each month.

I hope these hard truths are causing those imaginary light bulbs above your head to not only illuminate but burn so bright that you cannot ignore them. Since the majority of families—seventy five percent of American households—do not pay their credit card statements in full every month, the truth is inescapable: Americans can't handle their credit cards. The evidence is reflected in the fact that 34 million Americans pay their credit card late and 18 million have missed their payment entirely.

So, what can you do to turn things around? I suggest doing these things:

1. **Determine what it is that you actually owe.** Even though it's difficult to face your

financial obligations squarely, you must begin by tallying all your credit card debts. Start by looking at your monthly statement and add up the figure next to "Your Total Balance," the one that's much larger than "Minimum Amount Due."

Is it a scary number? Remember, anything over an aggregate number of $2,500 is cause for alarm. Credit card debt is a slippery slope—it doesn't take much credit card spending before you're in over your head.

2. **Take a credit card holiday.** There are several great reasons to stop charging and start paying by cash or personal check. For openers, it's going to be easier to get your credit card balances paid off when you're not adding to the balance each month. With steady progress made each month, you'll find that you're encouraged to keep chipping away at your debt.

As you embark on a credit card holiday, this would be a good time to take inventory of the cards in your purse or wallet. Most households have three to five credit and charge cards. This is no sin, of course, but having too much credit available has proven to be too great a temptation for many families.

Simplify life and scale back to one card, which you can use for emergencies or the online purchases that you absolutely have to make. One way to put your card "on ice" is to drop it in a bowl of water or Popsicle form and place it in your freezer. As for your other cards, can you cancel them? Sure you can, but canceling a credit card doesn't cancel your indebtedness.

3. **Start this month to pay off the lowest cards first.** Let's say you have a Macy's card with $338 in "hangover" charges. Your Best Buy card has $1,249—the amount left over from the purchase of a fancy flat-screen TV for the living room wall. And your Visa card has a honking $7,442 amount attached to your name. For the moment, you can allocate only $750 per month toward paying off these three bills.

    In concert with a reduced spending plan, send each creditor $250 a month. The minimum payment for the Visa charges is 2 percent, or around $148, so at least you'll receive credit for paying off some principal. Under this approach, the Macy's bill will be cleaned up in two months and the Best Buy card will take five months. With those victories boosting your confidence, you can turn your sights on wiping out that Visa balance.

If you're serious about really taking on that large Visa debt, your husband will have to work overtime or take a second job, and that's a real cost to the family. No matter what route you take, the days of lavish vacations are over.

Just as you don't get into debt overnight, you don't get *out* of debt overnight either.

FROM A POST ON MY BLOG . . .

She is an amazing woman who made an incredibly long comment on one of my financial posts. I'll call her Carla.

Carla does everything she can to live within her husband's income, even if it means sacrificing some of life's pleasures in life. Most women today simply put things on their credit card, thus digging their family deeper and deeper into debt. This is not a good way to live. Stuff will never bring happiness, and debt makes us slaves. Why not learn from this thrifty woman! Here, in Carla's own words, are some tips on how she does it:

> I breastfeed, use cloth diapers, cloth napkins, and diva cups, line dry our clothes, use a solar cooker, and burn wood for heat that we chop ourselves. We also cook on a wood stove and buy all clothes that we need second hand, except for socks and underwear. We pick as many wild blackberries as we can during the summer and freeze them.
>
> I make my own cleaning products, personal care products, and most condiments. I buy our staple foods in organic versions and make all of my own baked goods, treats, etc., from healthier ingredients.

We have slow dial-up Internet, no cable. No smart phones. No fancy tech gadgets. We do have newer vehicles, one that we are still paying on, and my hubby just bought a motorcycle for his commute because of the great gas mileage. We have a small backyard flock of chickens for eggs and for meat.

We use natural lighting and open the windows when it gets hot; we don't turn the A/C on until it gets to 85 degrees. We unplug all of our electronics when not in use, except for the fridge, upright freezer, alarm clock, and the electricity that runs our well pump. My kids don't do organized sports, but they are active. If they get a gift that they really don't like, we re-gift it to a friend. We don't do big birthday parties unless it's a milestone birthday, like turning ten or thirteen. We limit their Christmas gifts to five things: a want, a need, something to wear, a book, and a new Christmas ornament.

Vacations consist of visiting family in another state. We limit driving. We limit eating and impulse shopping at the supermarket; we stick to the grocery list. When the kids bathe, they share bathwater. I clean the shower with baking soda when I take my shower. We ask for new shoes from grandparents at birthdays and Christmas.

I work at our local YMCA to get a free family membership. We got rid of all of our carpeting so I could just sweep the floor and not have to use electricity to vacuum. We hardly ever, ever go to the movies, but if we do, we go to the second-run theater. We don't have expensive hobbies or participate in expensive activities. I sell things we no longer need on eBay. I could go on and on.

I'm always looking for ways to *save* money and stretch my husband's hard-earned income even more.

* * *

Moreover it is required in stewards, that a man be found faithful.
1 Corinthians 4:2 (KJV)

15

The Disciplined Mind: Trusting God and Doing Good

Life, besides being short, is difficult.

We will all suffer and go through trials. When I'm going through a tough time, often in pain, I try to remind myself that this would be a great time to discipline my mind. I rely on this Scripture to see me through:

> *Therefore, those also who suffer according to the will of God shall entrust their souls to a faithful Creator in doing what is right.*
>
> 1 Peter 4:19 (NASB)

I have physically suffered a great deal for the past twenty-five years. Life has been and still is very difficult. I believe that the reason I have not fallen into major depression is because I have disciplined my mind.

I understand that I must be continually transformed by the renewing of my mind, as Romans 12:2 teaches. My mind has kept me strong through my suffering. I remind myself who I am in Christ and that I can do all things because He strengthens me. When I am suffering or my mind begins to fill with anxious thoughts, I discipline my mind to dwell on the Word of God: the good, the lovely, the pure, and the things acceptable to Him.

I like the verse I quoted on the previous page because even though I have suffered much with several serious operations, I have a purpose. My purpose is to trust in the Lord, knowing He is taking care of me and doing good in me.

God is in control. Trust and do good.

Those two sentences of four words each are so simple to say yet so difficult to keep at the forefront of our thinking. Whatever state you are in and wherever you are, trust in the Lord and do good.

How can I do good when I'm in such physical pain and continue to go through rough patches? The Lord has given me the gift of teaching and has allowed me to minister to millions of women around the world through my blog—and I never have to leave my home. The Lord has been good to me, and when I'm feeling up to it, I enjoy spending my time mentoring women, helping my children with the grandchildren and their homes, or whatever the Lord puts in my path. I enjoy doing good, which is a fruit of the Holy Spirit and a result of trusting in Him.

Yes, it takes disciplining the mind to stay strong during trials. This is why you must stay in the Word and stay close to the Lord. He suffered greatly and knows what you're going through. He promises that He will never leave you or forsake you. You are called to dwell on the lovely and the good. Whenever you feel afraid, remind yourself of all of God's precious promises and rest in them.

Nothing is more destructive to the believer and non-believer alike than a sloppy, undisciplined mind. The battle is in the mind, for this is where we live each day. Ken likes to say that the mind is like a garden that grows good thoughts (fruit) and bad thoughts (weeds). Just as every garden must be tended to each day with the pulling of weeds and pruning of trees, so your mind must be actively tended to as well.

You must uproot the lies that are whispered into your mind and prune those thoughts to make them even more productive. You must find and dwell on the fruit of righteousness and good works so that you may glorify God with your mind. A mind left unattended and allowed to carry any—and all thoughts—is one in which even its owner will not want to dwell.

How we think is how we will behave. God made this clear as He says, "For as he thinks in his heart, so is he " (Proverbs 23:7, KJV). So how is your thought life? You cannot become a Transformed Wife without going to the source of the transformation, which is the battlefield of your mind.

God wants your mind fixed wholly and completely on Him, while the enemy wants your mind focused on selfishness and worldly things. We are to "bring into captivity every thought to the obedience of Christ" (2 Corinthians 10:5, KJV).

Did you catch the use of the word "every"? Yes, this means *every* thought your mind may be thinking, including thoughts that go against the knowledge and obedience to our Lord Jesus. So grab the bad thinking and tie it up with the Word of God, throwing the lies into the fiery furnace with the Father of Lies, where it belongs.

It's easy to be anxious and worried about many things. The news is always reminding us of the devastation going on around us in the world—from natural disasters like earthquakes and flooding, to terror attacks, indiscriminate bombings, and countless threats.

I don't believe we were created to be able to handle all of this devastation and bad news. There's not much we can do about it anyway, except to pray. Actually, we have *no* control over what's going on in the world. We only have control of ourselves and what we think, so I urge you to stop listening to the news and focus on your husband, your children, and your home instead. If you're troubled or worked up with the political scene, remember politics isn't our life! Jesus is our life.

You cannot be filled with joy if you're preoccupied by the ugly things in this world. You need to continually remind yourself what the Lord has done for you and the bright future that is awaiting you; if not here on this earth, then for eternity. You will always have hope. *Always.* As long as God is on His throne, there is hope. Our Savior is coming soon on His white stallion in the skies and, when He does appear, what will you then think of all those wasted thoughts? Don't allow those negative thoughts to rule your life and keep you from experiencing the joy that awaits you each day.

Hope is a wonderful thing. They say you can live thirty days without food, three days without water, and three minutes without air, but you can't survive a single second without hope. Every day, I hope that I'll feel better in the morning. Thankfully, since I'm usually a positive person, this hasn't been that difficult for me. If God tells me I can do something, I believe it. Because He promises to never leave me nor forsake me, He is with me and His promises are true today, yesterday, and forever.

LOOKING TO THINGS ABOVE

I know the Bible well. I've been reading God's Word almost daily since I turned eighteen, so it's been a long time. I usually read a section of Scripture slowly and pray through some verses, digesting them into my heart and mind. I want to grasp them for myself and try to comprehend what the Lord has done for me and who I am in Him.

I love learning things like how He wants us to keep our mind on things above, not on things of this earth, as the apostle Paul teaches us in Colossians 3:2. If I'm having a sleepless night, I'll pray for my husband, my children, my friends, and my neighbors by name. I'll pray for those in need and for those in pain. I'll try to get my mind off of myself and onto others so I can focus on doing something worthwhile. If you leave your mind unattended, it will quickly cycle lie after lie until you are paralyzed, unable to sort right thinking from wrong thinking.

At one time, I used to lay in my bed on restless nights trying to remember the sins I committed that day so I could ask for forgiveness. That was such a futile exercise since the moment I repented of my sins years ago and Jesus, as my Lord and Savior, forgave every single sin, past, present, and future.

Instead of dwelling on the sins in my life, I now thank the Lord for what He has done for me and through me. When I blow it at times, I thank Him that He forgave me thousands of years ago when He took all of my sins to the cross with Him. I thank Him that I died with Him, was buried with Him, and have risen with Him to share in all His glory at the right hand of God. This is just as God's Word promises in Colossians 3:1-4 and many other places in Scripture.

He has made us a new creature in Christ. All of these promises and realities should consume our minds, replacing our thinking about how bad the world is—and is becoming—or even the sins in and around us. We know how the story ends and who is left standing in victory, so we have no reason to worry. If you feel like you're getting anxious, remind yourself that you're called to trust in Him. Be anxious for nothing and then go out and do good.

Even if you're on a sick bed of suffering, you can do good. You can pray. You can be kind to those around you. You can preach Jesus by the way you live your life through the pain. This will speak volumes to others about the One who lives within you.

Always remember that God is viewing our individual lives based on what we *can* do for Him and His Kingdom, not what we *can't* do in life. The quadriplegic who can do nothing on her own to care for herself can still fit perfectly into God's plan. You do not have to be anything special, have any great intelligence, or do anything extraordinary to receive the bountiful blessings and promises God reserves for those who are faithful. You see, it's all about believing in His promises. Nothing more, nothing less. It's just being who God has made us to be and living for His glory.

Young mothers, I want to speak directly to your heart today and assure you that you can trust God with your children. He is there for them in the same way He's there for you and your husband. During this period of your life, raising children and being a good help meet is your biggest and most important calling. I hope you don't take that responsibility lightly. Your position is vital because you are the only one who can fulfill this role in the lives of those God has given you.

Being a good help meet and raising up the next generation of godly offspring has huge implications for generations to come. How you raise up your children will greatly impact how they raise their own children. You have the ability to set in motion generations of families who serve the Lord and bring Him glory. Do this with thankfulness and joy as this is your calling; this is where you will find your greatest reward here on earth and in the kingdom to come. After all, relationships are the most important things in life. Everything else pales in comparison.

Older women, choose to trust God as you age and let those wrinkles and gray hair come. Then go about doing good. Young women are desperate for older women to teach them and help them with their homes and families. There is good work waiting out there for you to do. There are so many young moms, as well as lonely and sick people, who could use a loving hand. They long for a relationship; someone to care for them in a difficult time of life. When you invest in these young ladies, be sure to plant seeds in them in such a way that they will, in turn, go out and do likewise as they grow in age and wisdom.

The great news is that you get to *choose* your attitude each and every day. Will you be joyful and trust in the Lord, or will you grumble and complain about your lot in life? Yes, the choice is that simple. If you choose to be grumpy, you're saying to others that you don't take God at His Word and doubt His ability to give you all you need for life and godliness. It's my hope that you will choose instead to put on a positive attitude that shines the light of Jesus on all you come across. The world desperately needs the kind of hope that can only be found in Christ, and you have the ability to point others to that hope through the choices you make every day.

Be sober in spirit so you can be alert to the dangers around you, protecting yourself and your family from the lies of Satan. Grow in the wisdom and the knowledge of the Lord so you can clearly distinguish between the lies of society versus the truth of God's Word.

Love your husband so that there will be peace and harmony in your home, and you can serve as an example of the unity between Christ and His church. We can represent strong, solid marriages to a society where this is becoming the exception rather than the norm. Show others that Christ is the glue that holds it all together.

How is a wife to acquire a disciplined and transformed mind? The place to begin is to go into your mind and uproot any lie that tells you that your husband is your enemy. This kind of message comes straight from the Deceiver.

Secondly, don't believe the lie that says the only accountability you need in order to keep a disciplined mind is just "you and God." Not only were you made to live within the body of Christ so that other believers can encourage, exhort, and rebuke you, but He also gave you a husband who knows your strengths and your weaknesses.

A husband has the best view of who you really are and can help you find the lies planted in the garden of your mind. He can help you uproot them, but only if you trust the Lord enough to believe that you are one with your husband and it's his job to lead you. It wasn't until I surrendered to this truth that I finally realized that God gave me my husband to help me on my journey to becoming the godly, submissive, and loving wife I was meant to be. Oh, how I wish I had learned long ago to stop seeing my godly husband in light of his faults and instead in light of the role God had given him to help me become who He wanted me to be.

If you want to be made whole and completely transformed by the promises in God's Word, then surrender the idea that your husband must be perfect before he can play a part in helping you change. Will you decide to let go and let God use whatever and whomever He chooses to transform you into the woman He wants you to be?

I sincerely hope so.

WORKING ON YOUR CHILDREN'S HEARTS

If you love your children and want them to grow up to represent the sweet aroma of Christ, you must discipline them and raise them in the nurture and admonition of the Lord. Work on their thinking more so than their behavior. Remember, all actions stem from either good thoughts or bad thoughts. Bad thoughts and lies are what push children toward destructive behaviors. The only way to change bad behavior is to change their thinking on the matter.

Ken and I spent many hours working on our children's thinking. Ken would take regular opportunities to talk to the kids about life and the Lord. He emphasized good thinking and bad thinking, and he helped distinguish between what is true and what is false. We took very seriously the admonition:

> "Hear, O Israel: The LORD our God is one LORD: And thou shalt love the LORD thy God with all thine heart, and with all thy soul, and with all thy might. And these words, which I command thee this day, shall be in thine heart: And thou shalt teach them diligently unto thy children, and shalt talk of them when thou sittest in thine house, and when thou walkest by the way, and when thou liest down, and when thou risest up. And thou shalt bind them for a sign upon thine hand, and they shall be as frontlets between thine eyes. And thou shalt write them upon the posts of thy house, and on thy gates."
>
> DEUTERONOMY 6:4-9 (KJV)

Can you not see that the battle for life and death is happening each and every moment of the day as we battle for truth? Jesus said, "The truth will set you free." Begin early in the lives of your children to teach them God's precepts and truth. Plant deeply in the gardens of their minds the promises of God, for His ways are always best. Man's ways and the ways of the world may have many earthly blessings, but they cannot compare to what God has in store for the one who believes Him.

Do your children know this at every age and in every stage of life? If not, vow to begin teaching them these truths this very day when you are sitting, walking, lying down, and rising up. Teach them about His goodness, His promises, and His perfect ways. Those precious little minds can be so easily influenced by the whispers of the world that beckon them to turn away from the truth of God's Word.

In the midst of that effort, be discreet and chaste so as to not cause others to stumble or give Satan a foothold in their lives. Draw others to Christ by your righteous behavior, which needs to look different from the world around you, and cause people to wonder what sets you apart.

It's your joy and gratitude that will make the Christian life come alive to your children. It's your love and submission to your husband that will model for them how they, as part of the body of Christ, are to love and submit to their Savior. Do your children see Christ living in you by the way you are obedient to the Word regarding submission? Be careful what you are modeling for your children as they will likely follow in your footsteps.

When you're a keeper at home, you need to always be ready to guard and protect your family from the enemy who aims to destroy. Be vigilant in protecting their eyes and minds. Nourish their bodies and souls with healthy things so they will be prepared for the spiritual battle they'll encounter in the world. Stage your home as a place of peace and order so that your family will have a refuge from the storm.

A house united stands, while a house divided falls. A house with one person in authority is strong, while a house with two heads destroys itself. God is a God of peace and order, not a God of strife. Remember, Jesus came to bring peace and He commands that we pursue it with all men. We should be known for being peacemakers, especially in our homes. In this way, we are a light to a lost world. Everyone is searching for peace, and you have the answer to what they seek. Never forget that the world is watching, and if you want to reach a lost world for Christ, you should begin in the home.

God gave the children of Israel the choice of life or death. We have been given that same choice. The question is: Will you choose life? A life that is abundant and free comes when you set your hearts and minds on Jesus, the author and perfector of our faith. May you allow Him to work in and through you to transform you into the likeness of His Son, Christ Jesus our Lord.

I realize this chapter has been a mini-sermon but it's a necessary message to hear. I close with this benedictory thought from Scripture:

> *"I call heaven and earth to record this day against you, that I have set before you life and death, blessing and cursing: therefore choose life, that both you and your seed may live: That you may love the LORD thy God, and that you may obey his voice, and that you may cleave unto him: for he is your life, and the length of your days: that you may dwell in the land which the LORD sware unto thy fathers, to Abraham, to Isaac, and to Jacob, to give them."*
>
> DEUTERONOMY 30:19-20 (KJV)

16
Clutter No More

Erin Harrison has a beautiful blog called Keeper of the Homestead and is the author of the book *Living Virtuously: Keeping Your Heart and Home.* She has five children and keeps a very clean and tidy home. She's a special friend of mine, and we enjoy talking on the phone whenever possible.

One time, while we were chatting, she told me her daughters were over at a neighbor's home cleaning the place for them, which really blessed me to hear. I find her posts detailing how she cleans her home to be informative, entertaining, and very helpful to women who weren't taught these skills growing up.

In the beginning, keeping a house spic and span wasn't natural for Erin, even though her mom maintained a spotless home. She was inspired to learn how to meticulously clean a home after deciding she was sick of living in a dirty, cluttered environment. Here are some of her own words about the importance of keeping a home that's inviting to live in:

> Having a clean home makes a heart cheery. If my home is a mess, I feel down and overwhelmed. I

stare at the clutter and clothes strewn about and wonder where to start.

A clean home is a welcoming home. People feel at ease when they step into a clean and orderly house. It's a sign that all is well when the home is in order.

I learned to like cleaning from my mother. Yes, I had to learn to appreciate the art of cleaning. Learning is a good thing; I've always believed we become proficient in tasks or things we like to do when we *want* to learn.

My mom was the best cleaner I knew of all the neighborhood moms. When you were in our home, everything smelled clean. Our home was inviting and restful. Nobody could joke that they would contract a disease by touching a countertop or using the guest bathroom.

I can remember walking barefoot throughout the house and not feeling a crumb. I appreciated what it took to maintain such a tidy environment because my mother taught me how to clean properly, just as her mother taught her when Mom was growing up. I'm proud that I have passed on the skills that I learned from my mother to the next generation.

And then there are the homes we've all been to . . . the homes that are pigpens, as my mother used to call them.

This isn't any great revelation, but I've noticed that a mother who isn't concerned about a clean home will produce daughters who aren't concerned either. They don't mind, for some reason, being surrounded by dirt, clutter, and filth. In fact, they do not see the dirt—and if they do see dirt, they don't care. The house smells foul, and the floors are almost as bad as those found in a barnyard stable. They have dogs living in the home that shed and leave messes that aren't cleaned up, which is really gross. In those situations, I breathe out of my mouth to avoid the icky smells or look for an excuse to leave. It's unbelievably disgusting.

When my children were babies, I would take them on "play dates" to other homes, but if the home was a mess, I worried about the grime, the germs, and the choking hazards. I didn't want to leave any of my children on the floor because I could see the dust and dirt everywhere. That grime would coat my children's hands and feet as well as their clothing. I always had an uneasy feeling during those play dates. I didn't want to make the hostess feel badly, but I'm sure there were times when the expression on my face revealed that I was extremely uncomfortable.

Speaking of filthy, I have to talk about toilets. A home that is rarely cleaned will always have bathrooms with dirty toilets. I don't think I have to get too descriptive here, but I think we can agree that dirty bathrooms contain a strong smell of urine. That's because guys don't always have the best aim and splash urine down the side of the toilet to the floor around the base. The odors get trapped there.

Listen, I understand that cleaning toilets qualifies for Worst Job Ever. But I'll give you a little hint: if you clean your bathroom and toilets regularly—and by that I mean every few days and no more than a week in between—the distasteful job isn't so overwhelming. If your children are older, this is an important chore to teach them. If you don't teach them how and why it's important to clean toilets, who will?

Talk to them about a recent restaurant you may have visited. Explain how a clean bathroom in a restaurant is often a sign of a clean kitchen—and vice versa. If a clean bathroom smells nice and is spotless, you know the management cares about every detail.

The kitchen is another place that seems to attract disorder. Just as it takes work to cook, it's sometimes just as much work to clean up after the food is prepared. You have to stay on top of the pots and pans as well as the plates, glasses, and cutlery. There's nothing more discouraging than seeing a kitchen sink filled with dirty dishes, so either rinse them off and get them into the dishwasher or get them washed.

All it takes is a little elbow grease, and before you know it, kitchen clean-up will be over.

NO EXCUSES PLEASE

We've all had friends who've said that a dirty home is a happy home. It's funny how the only people who say that have a really messy house.

I've had some women tell me that they would feel stressed and in a bad mood if they had to keep their home clean. They say they don't respond well to the pressure to keep a tidy house. My question is *why*? Why would cleaning a home make anyone stressed when the end result—a clean, uncluttered environment—*reduces* stress?

Even though I grew up in a clean home, I wasn't the perfect housewife early on. In fact, I was a bit of a slob, so I knew all the excuses . . . *I'm too tired . . . it's too late . . . there are too many other things to do.*

I'm glad I put my excuses aside because, years later, I find cleaning to be personally satisfying. It feels good to look around my home and see clean floors and a shipshape kitchen. It's awesome to go into one of my bathrooms and see clean floors and smell a pleasing scent instead of the rank odor of urine.

On the occasions when I got behind on my housework and my home became dirty and cluttered, the stress nearly crushed me. I felt unmotivated, lazy, and just plain overwhelmed just looking around at the mess. I got nasty and grouchy when my house was not clean.

Contrary to stereotypes you see in movies and on TV, men actually love a clean and orderly home. After being gone all day at work, they enjoy coming home to a fresh environment. A spic-and-span home sets the mood for a relaxing evening for him to unwind with his family. Even if some men say they don't care about a tidy home, they will agree that order and cleanliness are *always* more pleasant than disorder.

Some women argue that cleaning takes them away from spending quality time with their children. Hey, you can spend a lot of quality time with your children by cleaning *with* them! Straightening up the house was part of our family time. As soon as my kids could walk, they were my cleaning buddies. Sure, they couldn't do much and the tasks I gave them were small, but that wasn't the point. They learned early on that cleaning was a part of daily living. This wasn't a huge mountain to climb—just a few short steps each morning.

The attitude that I tried to get across to our kids was this: *We all live here, so we all clean here.* The way I look at things, the more children you have, the more cleaning buddies you can call upon. The older kids can team up with the younger children during chore time to pass on their skills. That's a win/win situation—building relationships while creating a haven of refreshing beauty.

A guiding verse from Colossians 3:23 (NASB) is applicable here: "Whatever you do, do your work heartily, as for the Lord and not to men . . ."

LEARNING TO CLEAN

You can learn to be a good cleaner. It's not a gift. It's not even a personality trait. It is a skill—and a good thing to know how to do, especially because God calls us to be keepers of the home.

I recommend that you check out Erin Harrison's blog at *http://www.keeperofthehomestead.com/blog* and pick up more great tips on how to keep your home clean and organized. You can also find links to a whole series of videos filled with practical advice on how to best clean your home.

I'm fascinated, and yet extremely sad, whenever I watch one of those "hoarder" shows on cable TV. Often, piles of clothes, household items, and junk fill every nook and cranny of the home. Hallways are nearly blocked, except for a narrow path to navigate between the rooms in which they live. The kitchen resembles a garbage dump from all the fast-food boxes and packaging strewn about in piles. The hoarders—usually women—can barely sleep in their bedroom or living room and are nearly buried alive by the piles of junk around them.

I once visited a woman I knew who wasn't quite a major-league hoarder but she was close to being called up from the minors to the majors. I remember having to walk through tiny rows from room to room because there was so much stuff piled up high. I involuntarily shuddered . . . living like that would make me depressed. I like as little clutter as possible and plenty of free, open space. I even love an empty drawer or two!

Besides watching a hoarder episode every now and then on cable, I also tune in to shows about renovating older homes. Each time I watch, I'm struck by how tiny the closets are. Obviously, people didn't own that many clothes sixty, eighty, or a hundred years ago. There was the Sunday suit or dress, some work clothes, one or two pairs of shoes, and that was it. Contrast that to the *House Hunters* shows these days where the couples have to have "his and her" walk-in closets that are as big as my old bedroom growing up.

Do we really need so many clothes? I rarely even notice what someone wears and, if I do, those clothes don't make that friend, or acquaintance, more special to me. God's Word teaches us in 1 Timothy 2:9 that women are not to adorn themselves with expensive clothing because He cares much more about our behavior than our clothing, elaborate hairstyling, gold jewelry, and fine pearls. Our value does not come from an abundance of possessions either.

With regards to possessions, if you haven't worn something for a year or so, toss it or give it away, unless it's an expensive dress used for occasions like a wedding, a special event, or funeral. Take a look around your closet: Do you really need that many shoes and purses? I have two purses—my everyday one and one for special occasions. I probably own about eight pairs of shoes. I try to stay away from malls and outlet stores since I know, deep in my heart, that I have plenty of clothes and there are so many better ways to spend our money, like helping others.

It's all about reducing clutter in your life. If you're looking to dive deeper into the topic, then check out my favorite book on clutter, which is *Clutter's Last Stand: It's Time to De-Junk Your Life!* by Don Aslett, who says that cleaning junk out of your life can be exhilarating.

I wholeheartedly agree.

FROM A POST ON MY BLOG . . .

When it comes to hoarding and filling our lives with "stuff," God calls us not to store our treasures on earth.

Everything on earth is going to burn up, and I mean everything. Therefore, I don't get too sentimental about buying or collecting things because it'll all be gone—one way or another—very soon.

Since I know that stuff rusts, falls out of fashion, or is

surpassed by the 2.0 version, I have no problem letting it go. I like giving away my old stuff. Maybe someone else can get some use out of those items. This confirms, as least to me, why there's no reason to hoard or think about how much stuff you can accumulate. It's all going to burn.

So where are you storing your treasures?

* * * * * * * * * * * * * * * * * * * *

Do not store up for yourselves treasures on earth, where moth and rust destroy, and where thieves break in and steal. But store up for yourselves treasures in heaven, where neither moth nor rust destroys, and where thieves do not break in and steal: for where your treasure is, there your heart will be also.

MATTHEW 6:19-21 (NASB)

17
Serving Healthy Foods Means Healthy Families

A Transformed Wife wants to take care of her family to the best of her ability, and a big part of doing this is preparing and serving healthy, nutritious foods.

What about your children? Are you pleased with their weight and fitness, or could they be doing better? As their mom, you're their health coach—the parent responsible for their well-being. They're depending on you.

Remember, I'm a health nut and was raised this way by my mom. She trained me in the way I should go and, when I grew up, I did not depart from what was good and what was healthy to eat. I eat organic food as often as possible since I was raised on it and know that I don't want to consume foods with preservatives and toxic chemicals.

Conventional crops are sprayed with powerful toxic chemicals to rid the fruits and vegetables of pests. Unfortunately, these chemicals stay in the food, which is then consumed. On top of that, the chemicals end up destroying the health of the soil so that in subsequent years, the new crops don't have the same amount of healthy nutrients. Eventually, the foods that come from the depleted ground are less nutritious.

Another point is that organic produce tastes much better than non-organic. When I was growing up, my dad would have my mom close her eyes and have her taste an organic apple and a conventionally grown apple. Mom could always tell the difference. I would much rather eat fruits, vegetables, and meat just the way God created them than consume foods filled with toxic chemicals not fit for the human body.

But Lori, organic foods cost more—sometimes a lot more. How can we afford to eat healthier?

Shopping at farmer's markets and buying in bulk in the organic section of your local supermarket or warehouse club is a great place to start. These days, because of the rising popularity of organic food, grocery stores often have "loss leaders" on organic items, which is a good time to stock up.

Another great idea, if you have the space, is raising your own chickens and cultivating a backyard garden. Producing your own food is a wonderful project to be involved in for your family. Even if you have a postage stamp-sized backyard, you can still have clay pots filled with some type of fruit or vegetable.

In our Southern California backyard, we have apple, lemon, orange, fig, lemon, and peach trees, for which I'm thankful. I used to garden a lot more when I had a healthy neck and would grow all types of vegetables.

I still haven't forgotten how my mom had a huge garden when I was growing up, and the meals she made from our garden were my favorite. There were times when I would have fresh corn on the cob or a green salad with large tomatoes. Other days, she prepared cucumbers, snap peas, and other veggies picked that day. If you have a productive garden, you can can your produce when everything is ripe at the same time.

But if having your own garden isn't possible or practical, know that even the major supermarket chains are stocking organic foods because of its popularity. I love how Costco now carries a lot of organic food, and so does another shopping favorite of mine—Trader Joe's.

We have a health food store near us that sells great organic produce from local farmers. This is where I get most of my produce, but many cities and towns across America and all over the world have farmer's markets, often on weekends, that offer a great variety of freshly grown and pesticide-free food.

Be creative and ask the Lord for wisdom in this area since toxic chemicals are known to cause cancer. As a wife and mother, you should do everything in your power to make sure your family eats as healthy as they can. If there is no way you can afford organic food or grow a garden, shop the outer walls of the supermarket—where the produce, meat, and dairy products are—and stay away from the boxed and canned foods found in the main aisles.

Also, try to not buy fruits and vegetables with the most pesticide residue, unless they are organic. Known as the "Dirty Dozen," they are:

- apples
- peaches
- celery
- potatoes
- cherry tomatoes
- snap peas
- spinach
- cucumbers

- strawberries
- grapes
- nectarines
- sweet bell peppers

Beyond the Dirty Dozen are the "Clean 15," which are fruits and veggies that you can even eat from conventional farmers because they are not sprayed as heavily with pesticides. They are:

- onions
- avocados
- sweet corn
- pineapple
- mango
- sweet peas
- eggplant
- cauliflower
- asparagus
- kiwi
- cabbage
- watermelon
- grapefruit
- sweet potatoes
- honeydew melon

CLOSER TO HOME

My children were raised on healthy food, so they love large salads at mealtime. For mid-morning or afternoon snacks, I would prepare various fruits and nuts. Since I didn't allow them to be picky eaters, they all grew up to enjoy most foods. A mother has a lot of control in how she raises her children and what they like to eat. Take the opportunity to raise them to love healthy food.

My favorite food is a big salad with several types of lettuce, flavorful tomatoes, chunks of avocado, and salted sunflower seeds. I love roasted chicken, wild-caught fish, farm-fresh eggs, nuts, yams, baked potatoes, and carrots, cucumbers, and beets that are fermented.

Soon after my son Ryan met Erin, he described me to Erin as a mother who made nutritious food and quoted a lot of Bible verses. Right on both counts!

I figure if God made food a certain way for us to eat, man can't improve upon it. This is why I disdain all processed foods like boxed cereals, Pop Tarts, crackers, canned fruits in heavy syrups, chicken nuggets, and fast foods. Even though I've had my share of health problems over the years, I know they would have been a lot worse if I was a junk food fan. Just like I don't like junk television, junk movies, or junk anything, I don't like junk food.

Learn how to make meals out of healthy ingredients such as homemade chicken broth, organic chicken, wild-caught fish, or whatever your family likes. There are many good recipes on the Internet, but I invite you check out my family-tested recipes on my blog at www.lorialexander.blogspot.com.

Everything I make is delicious, but don't take my word for it—give my recipes a try. And please don't say you can't cook. Yes, practice helps, but as I like to say, if you can read, you can cook. You can learn to make healthy meals that your family will like and are so good for them!

Finally, let me share some advice to mothers who are unable to nurse their babies and dislike the idea of giving their baby formula, which is a processed food. When my grandma couldn't breastfeed one of her babies, she bought a goat and gave her child raw goat's milk, a practice that dates back to ancient times.

Goat's milk is an easily digestive protein that does not contain the same complex proteins found in cow's milk. In addition, a baby's stomach can fully digest goat's milk in as little as twenty minutes, while pasteurized cow's milk can take as long as eight hours since its fats and protein are considerably larger in size.

I'm not suggesting that you raise goats in your backyard, but goat's milk is readily available in health food stores, so feeding your infant goat's milk is definitely an idea worth checking out. We just found a little store that sells goat's milk ice cream in all kinds of flavors. It was delicious! Hopefully, this will become a new trend.

A last thought on milk: I'm not a fan of soy milk, which is full of estrogen. Estrogen is not good for babies, especially boy babies.

TURNING A PAGE

I shudder to think what my health would be like if I didn't pay close attention to what I eat. My problems started at a young age when I ran full speed into a plate-glass sliding door, falling on my back. Then I was driving one time when my car was smashed between two eighteen-wheel semis. I've had health issues with my head and neck ever since then, so it's imperative that I do what I can to stay healthy.

A lifetime of being careful about my diet has allowed me to be healthy despite the difficult circumstances of accidents, parasites, and tumors. My blood workup is always great, and my organs work well. I'm hopeful that my poor pituitary gland, which has been radiated to the maximum allowable limit, will continue to do its job.

My focus on good health continued when our children came along. As the kids grew, I often referred to a book by Dr. Robert Mendelsohn, a longtime pediatrician who advises parents on home treatment and diagnosis of colds, flues, illnesses, and allergies. Titled *How to Raise a Healthy Child in Spite of Your Doctor*, Dr. Mendelsohn helped me to understand whether something was an emergency or not. I loved his message that pharmaceutical drugs weren't the answer to everything. He knew the power of the wonderful immune system our Creator designed for us.

Since all drugs have side effects, we rarely gave our children any drugs. Doctors, being human, aren't infallible so keeping a balanced perspective on their role is important. Most are taught to prescribe pharmaceutical drugs and perform surgery, and anything else—such as employing a holistic or homeopathic approach—is "outside the box." Today's doctors aren't taught about keeping a healthy immune system and fighting diseases without drugs. While doctors are great for emergency situations, they aren't as great at healing chronic conditions or diseases.

I'm also aware that we can do everything "right" yet still suffer debilitating illness. Some diseases are caused by the toxicity of our air, water, and food supply—lead poisoning being an example. When we are unable to discover a cause for an illness or a chronic condition, focus on trusting the Lord with the situation. He tells us that all we have to do is ask Him for wisdom, and He will give it.

There's growing concern about the dangers of invisible non-ionizing radiation from microwaves, cell phones, and cell towers. My attitude is that we live in a decaying world that will be folded up for good one day. All we can do is our best with the knowledge and wisdom that we have and then depend upon the Lord for His protection and provision.

It may surprise you to discover that the air inside a home is often *more* toxic than the air outside, so I suggest you open your windows as often as possible to let in fresh air. Most women clean floors, furniture, and countertops with chemicals cleaners, which means all those surfaces are toxic and the air gets stagnant if the windows are never opened. And please get rid of those scented candles, unless they are naturally scented. Otherwise, you are further polluting your indoor air. Instead buy some houseplants, which are fantastic air filters.

I've always been grateful that we've lived in a sunny home. I don't like curtains on the windows, except for bedrooms, since they prevent the sun from shining into our living quarters. Not only are the sun's rays a great sanitizer—you have to be my age to remember when mothers hung out their clothes to dry—but getting sunlight is extremely important for our bodies because of the way the skin synthesizes vitamin D from the ultraviolet rays of sunlight. Exposure to the sun is a significant source of vitamin D, which plays a role in immunity and blood cell formation and is also needed for adequate blood levels of insulin.

Vitamin D experts say that more than 90 percent of Americans have a vitamin D deficiency, so it's likely that you're among that group. You can meet your recommended daily allowance of vitamin D by going out into the sun for ten minutes each day, although you should be aware that sunlight exposure from November to February is often insufficient to produce significant vitamin D synthesis in the skin. Still, no matter what month of the year it is, taking yourself and your children for a walk to soak up some rays will provide an excellent as well as free health benefit.

ABOUT THOSE HOUSEHOLD CLEANERS

*A*voiding toxic chemicals and saving money is why I make almost all of my own household cleaners. They are simple to make, easy to use, and I don't have to worry about adding more toxic chemicals to our home and further burdening our immune systems.

For my laundry, I use the following recipe for washing detergent and wash almost everything in warm water. My washing detergent doesn't dissolve that great in cold water, so you will have to take a scoop of it and dissolve it into some hot water before pouring it into the washing machine if you're doing a cold water wash.

Here's my recipe:

WASHING MACHINE DETERGENT

1 box Borax
1 4 lb. box of baking soda
1 box of washing soda
3 bars Fels-Naptha soap
5 1/2 cups OxiClean

Directions:

Grate the soap finely in a food processor. Mix in a bit of the washing soda to prevent the soap from getting sticky. Combine all the ingredients in a 5-gallon bucket and stir well. Use 1 to 2 tablespoons per load.

The cost comes out to about three cents a load and even works in cold water with whites and darks as long as you follow my tip about dissolving the powder in hot water prior to washing. You'll be surprised by how clean your clothes can become. As for the ingredients, you can find Fels-Naptha at Walmart or Ace Hardware. If you can't find washing soda, spread baking soda on a cookie sheet and bake it at 350 degrees for 30 minutes. Presto . . . you have washing soda that works great.

When I'm done making my washing detergent, I fill a glass container and leave it on my dryer with a tablespoon-measuring cup so I'm ready to go. Make sure you keep your detergent sealed or it may start clumping up.

I also make my own all-purpose cleaner for around the home. The recipe is quite simple:

ALL-PURPOSE HOME CLEANER

Directions:

Get a spray bottle and fill it one-third full of vinegar and one-third hydrogen peroxide. Fill the rest with water. Add a squirt of dish soap and a few drops of an essential oil if you like.

This home cleaner is cheap and works great. If you want to clean with just water, try Norwex cloths, which make cleaning easy and work better than any cleaning cloths I have ever used. I also use Bar Keepers Friend cleaner to scour my sinks, tubs, and toilet bowls.

I shop for non-toxic lotions, shampoo, and make-up as well. Anything that you put on your skin will be absorbed into your body and your bloodstream very quickly. I also make my own deodorant, which works great and is easy to make. Here is the recipe for my deodorant, but I don't use extra virgin coconut oil because it smells like coconut. Instead, I use regular coconut oil, which is anti-fungal and anti-bacterial. Bacteria is what causes the smell under your arms, and coconut oil kills the bacteria naturally.

HOMEMADE DEODORANT

Melt in a small saucepan:
6 tablespoons of coconut oil

Directions:
Stir in 1/4 cup of baking soda and 1/4 cup of cornstarch. Mix together well. As it cools off, it hardens. Store in a small glass bowl.

If you don't want your shirts, blouses, or tops to get greasy, use a towel to wipe your underarms to get off any excess oil before putting on your tops.

ALKALINE VERSUS ACIDIC FOODS

A diet consisting of meat, grains, and dairy products tends to increase the amount of acidity in the body, which is why it's important to balance your diet with alkaline-rich foods such as vegetables, fruits, and nuts. It's all about having the right pH balance.

Babies are born alkaline, which means their pH balance is optimal. Newborns have pretty pink tongues, and breast-fed babies keep them. Formula-fed babies develop a white coating on their tongues because they become more acidic. As we grow older, disease breeds in acidic bodies. When you die, you are very acidic. Therefore, the key is to stay as alkaline as possible.

In terms of overall nutrition, a basic rule of thumb is that most raw foods cause our bodies to become more alkaline, which is beneficial. Processed and cooked foods, as I have mentioned previously, are more likely to turn our bodies acidic. My recommendation is to feed your family, and yourself, as many alkaline foods as possible to keep a strong immune system.

Some ways I make sure I get plenty of alkaline-producing food into my body is to drink a big glass of warm lemon water or lemonade first thing when I wake up. All you have to do is juice one or two lemons and add to filtered water or sparkling water, plus a little Stevia, and you're ready to go. Your body has been fasting overnight, so this is a great beverage to kick-start your day.

Coffee, the most popular breakfast drink in the world, is very acidic and hard on your adrenal glands. The caffeine in coffee is a mood-altering drug that has side effects: insomnia, nervousness and restlessness, upset stomach, nausea and vomiting, increased heart and breathing rate, and headaches. Drinking coffee is also highly addictive.

I don't think sport drinks like Gatorade or energy drinks like Red Bull are any better. When I work out and sweat like crazy, I stir the juice of one whole lemon or lime into a glass of sparkling or regular water, add a dash air-dried sea salt, a few drops of Stevia, and a few cubes of ice. These ingredients help restore my electrolytes and minerals. My "sports drink" tastes similar to Gatorade but is much healthier.

Once a day I make sure I prepare a big salad with all kinds of greens and vegetables of all different colors. A green smoothie is also a great way to make sure you get your vegetables and fruit. Kids seem to love healthy smoothies, so if you have children turning up their noses to what's good for them, consider making them an awesome smoothie each day.

Children also love fruit, so make that their snack instead of store-bought cookies or chips. Apples, peaches, grapes, bananas, and melon were my children's favorite snacks growing up. Give them healthy food while they are young so they will have a taste for it when they are adults.

I encourage you to study nutrition, which is easy to do with all the health-oriented websites available today. And I encourage you—the keeper of the home and all that it entails with the children—to get as fit and healthy as you can. In fact, being healthy is one of the most wonderful gifts you can give your children. Mark my words: being healthy is a lot cheaper than being ill in the long run.

One thing that people forget is that most cancers and common diseases can be prevented. We've all had a family member or friend who learned he or she has cancer at way too young an age. I just met a woman in my Bible study who is in severe, constant pain as a result of chemotherapy and radiation. She lives on morphine. She told me she's sorry she went the chemotherapy-and-radiation route because of how those treatments ravaged her body. Live and eat in a way to prevent cancer and other diseases.

When you and your family have your health, you're better able to live a full and rich life and, more importantly, serve where the Lord calls you. When you and your family are overweight, slowed down by diabetes and other diseases, life becomes more burdensome, and your ability to live to the fullest and serve to the fullest is diminished. If you're struggling with weight, the book *Trim Healthy Mama*, authored by Pearl Barrett and Serene C. Allison, has received rave reviews by women who comment on my blog.

Remember though, that even if you lose your health, you still have Jesus if you are a believer. Having Him is the only thing that matters in the end.

FROM A POST ON MY BLOG . . .

Since I love teaching about pregnancy and having children, I thought this blog would be fitting:

As many of you know, I have four children but I've been pregnant five times. My first pregnancy ended in a miscarriage, so I was thrilled to finally be pregnant again. All I ever wanted in life was to be a wife and mom. Since I hadn't been too sick with my first pregnancy, I was happy to be sick with my second one. I had heard that the sicker you are, the healthier your baby is going to be. (I don't think this is the case for all women, but it seemed to be for me.)

I didn't go for a doctor's appointment until I was almost five months along since I felt the less intervention, the better. Back then, doctors didn't require much testing during pregnancy. I liked that since I never would have had an abortion anyway. I only had one sonogram, but we didn't want to know the baby's sex. I was content waiting until the moment the baby was born to learn if we had a boy or a girl.

If you're thinking about getting pregnant or are pregnant, here are some things I learned:

1. **Make sure you get plenty of rest.** Even when I was working, during my breaks I would rest my head on the table. When I got home, I took time to lie down. There's lot is going on in your body while you are pregnant. You're creating another human being, remember! When I was home full time with my last two pregnancies, I would put the children down for a nap and then rest while listening to praise music.

2. **Make sure you are eating as healthy as you can.** When I had morning sickness during the first few months, I lived on raw almonds, bananas, and baked potatoes with avocado. It was about all I could stomach, but at least it was nourishing food. It's important to eat healthy fats like olive oil, butter, and coconut oil (the latter is known to prevent stretch marks), protein from healthy sources, and plenty of fruits and vegetables. These should be your main source of nutrition.

3. **Stay away from junk food.** Sugar, caffeine, processed foods, and white flour are not nourishing at all and can actually destroy your health. I never had a problem with retention of water (known as an edema) since I didn't eat any junk. I gained around twenty pounds with each of my children, and they all arrived into this world at around the seven-pound mark.

One time, I remember reading about a mother of ten children who noticed that each child was getting bigger, plus she got gestational diabetes. She concluded it was due to eating too much junk!

4. **Drink a lot of water.** Since the volume of blood and water is going to be much greater while housing a baby, you need to make sure you are drinking plenty of good filtered water.

5. **Always wear comfortable clothing and shoes.** It's not worth backaches and being uncomfortable to look in-style and fancy. You don't want to do anything that risks the health of you or your baby by wearing something that is too tight or uncomfortable.

6. **Try natural remedies for sicknesses or pain.** I have used many different treatments for my illnesses and pain that didn't include drugs and were not harmful to my health. I was watching Dr. Oz one time, and he had a doctor on his show who said that all drugs are toxic to the human body since they are chemicals with side effects. Dr. Oz agreed and said that since doctors are taught this in medical school, drugs should be a last resort. So know this: since drugs are toxic to the human body, anything you ingest *will* go to your baby. For example, Zofran, a prescription drug used to prevent nausea and vomiting, is sometimes used for morning sickness, but did you know about all the side effects from using it? If at all possi-

ble, use essential oils, supplements, foods, etc. to deal with what ails you, but make sure they are safe for pregnant women before taking them.

7. **At the end of a long day, try putting your feet up at night.** My feet never did get swollen since I didn't retain water, but pregnancy is still hard on the feet because of the extra weight you're carrying.

After the kids are put down and the kitchen is cleaned up, find a comfortable place with lots of pillows so you can rest. Read a good book or watch an uplifting television show. Dwell on the lovely and the good. You don't need to know about all the bad things happening in the world.

8. **Take one day at a time.** Pregnancy, for most women, is not that easy because of morning sickness, back pain, contractions, etc. Try not to worry and choose to rest in the Lord for strength. I was quite sick with my fourth baby and had three young children to care for at the time, but the Lord brought me through. He is faithful to do this for His children.

9. **Try to keep your joy!** I know pregnancy can be difficult, but what a joy it is when you hold that precious baby in your arms. There's truly no greater joy than to have children walking in Truth.

> *Whenever a woman is in labor she has pain, because her hour has come; but when she gives birth to the child, she no longer remembers the anguish because of the joy that a child has been born into the world.*
>
> John 16:21 (NASB)

18
A Way to a Man's Heart . . .

. . . is through his stomach.

There's some truth to that old saying, which is why fixing nourishing food for your family is a must. My blog has all my favorite, time-tested recipes, but I thought I'd share a few here to give you a taste for what I like to cook for my husband and family.

My approach to meal planning is to have a small repertoire of healthy and delicious "go-to" meals and repeat them frequently. Too often woman are burdening themselves by continually making something new and different. There's no need to reinvent the wheel when it comes to preparing healthy meals.

The following recipes are easy to make and healthy to eat. Though I'm not a gourmet cook, I do like food to taste good and be good for you. Without further adieu, roll up your sleeves and get cooking!

ALISA'S SUPER MOIST ROAST CHICKEN

Ingredients
    1 whole organic chicken
    1/4 to 1/3 cup melted ghee or butter
    thyme
    garlic powder
    sea salt
    pepper

Directions

    Preheat oven to 300°. Remove anything inside the chicken. Rinse the chicken and pat dry with several paper towels. Place the chicken in a large baking dish or oven-proof pan with a lid. Use your hands to coat the chicken with melted ghee. Sprinkle the entire chicken with thyme, garlic powder, salt, and pepper. Place it in the oven, covered, for 2 hours.

    Remove the lid, increase the temperature to 350°, and cook for an additional 30 minutes. After the chicken is cooked, drain off all the liquid into a glass jar. Once the liquid cools, put the lid on and refrigerate for later. Allow the chicken to sit for 20 minutes before eating.

    Note: I melt ghee, which is clarified butter, in a stainless steel measuring cup.

CHICKEN ROSEMARY STEW

Ingredients
   8 organic chicken thighs (breasts are okay too)
   rosemary sprigs
   melted ghee or butter
   organic thyme
   organic garlic powder
   Real Salt or Celtic Sea Salt
   organic pepper

Directions

Preheat oven to 425 degrees. In a cast-iron skillet (or any old skillet if you don't have a cast iron one), coat the bottom of pan with olive oil.

Salt and pepper 8 chicken thighs with the skin and bones. Cook each side in oil for 8 minutes, then remove from pan. Sauté 1 chopped up carrot, onion, and 2 celery in the fat for 10 minutes. Add 2 sprigs of rosemary. Squeeze 1 lemon into the pan and scrape the bottom of the pan to get all the yummy stuff off. Place the chicken on top of all the vegetables. Add 2 cups chicken broth, preferably homemade. Bring to a boil, then put it in the oven for 40 minutes. When cooked, place chicken and vegetables over brown rice.

Note: I usually use chicken thighs but you can use chicken breasts or legs if you prefer. The thighs and legs have extra fat that makes it taste real good. If you do not have a cast-iron skillet, you will have to transfer the whole dish to an oven-proof dish. Remember to save all of the uneaten skin and bones for making bone broth. Store the bones and skin in the freezer if you're not making broth immediately. Lastly, remove the whole rosemary sprigs before serving.

HEARTY CHICKEN PARMESAN

Ingredients
  6-8 boneless, skinless organic chicken breasts cut into long, narrow strips
  3 slices of whole wheat bread or homemade bread
  1 cup of Parmesan cheese
  1 teaspoon garlic powder
  1 teaspoon sea salt
  paprika
  several stems of parsley or cilantro, if desired
  1 stick of butter

Directions
  In a blender or Cuisinart, add 3 slices of whole wheat bread or homemade bread, 1 cup of Parmesan cheese, 1 teaspoon garlic powder, 1 teaspoon sea salt, and parsley or cilantro. Blend until crumbly. Melt one stick of butter and place it into a large pan. Lay the chicken on top of the butter. Spread the bread mixture over the chicken. Sprinkle with paprika.

  Bake at 350 degrees for 45 minutes. If the chicken starts getting too brown, cover it with tin foil.

  Note: I put Hearty Chicken Parmesan on top of my Homemade Spaghetti Sauce and whole wheat pasta with more Parmesan cheese. This is an easy meal that's great for the family and any company we have over.

SPICY SPAGHETTI SAUCE

Ingredients
   2 lbs. of ground turkey or beef
   2 tablespoons of olive oil
   1 large onion, chopped
   minced cloves of garlic
   25 oz. jar of a marinara or spaghetti sauce
   2 14.5 oz. cans of diced tomatoes
   1 14.5 oz. can of fire-roasted tomatoes
   2 tablespoons dried oregano
   2 tablespoons dried basil
   1-2 tablespoons of sugar or a small squirt of Stevia (optional)
   cayenne pepper
   sea salt
   pepper

Directions

Brown the meat in 2 tablespoons of olive oil. Salt the meat with 1 teaspoon of salt and 1 teaspoon of pepper. Add 1 large chopped onion and cook for 15 minutes. Add several minced cloves of garlic (or more if you love garlic). Add marinara or spaghetti sauce, diced tomatoes, fire-roasted tomatoes, dried oregano, dried basil, a pinch of cayenne, and sugar (or Stevia) to taste.

Simmer 2-3 hours uncovered. Start slowly adding more salt, pepper, cayenne, and sugar until seasoned to your liking.

Note: We use this sauce on whole wheat pasta with fresh Parmesan cheese. I like to add fresh mushrooms and broccoli during the last half-hour of cooking.

TURKEY AND BROWN RICE CHILI

Ingredients
   3/4 lb. of organic ground turkey (or beef)
   1 onion, chopped
   1 tablespoon of olive oil
   2 15-oz. cans of diced tomatoes
   2 15-oz. cans of black beans
   2 teaspoons chili powder
   1 teaspoon cumin
   ½ teaspoon sea salt
   1 tablespoon sugar

Directions

In a large saucepan, sauté ground turkey (or beef) in olive oil. When the meat is browned, add chopped onion. Cook 15 minutes, then add diced tomatoes, black beans, chili powder, cumin, sea salt, and sugar.

Let it simmer on the stove for an hour or put it in a slow cooker for 4-6 hours uncovered. Season to taste.

Note: We like to well-season this chili recipe, which is a staple in our home during the cool months. I usually serve the chili over brown rice that has been cooked in chicken broth.

AND FOR YOUR NEXT MEAL . . .

If you would like many more recipes, please go to my blog at www.lorialexander.blogspot.com. You'll find many great-tasting recipes that your husband and family will love!

19

The Power to Become a Transformed Wife

Jesus.
He is all we need.

I thought about just leaving it at that, but I think it's important that you hear Ken speak of the transformation—later in this chapter—that he has seen in me as we have journeyed through thirty-five years of life and marriage.

I am dramatically different than I was when we first married, and even more so these past fifteen years as I have put into practice all that God asks of me. I am living proof that knowing what the Bible teaches and actually living it out are two different things. Once a woman puts her life into the hands of God and allows Him to change her, these two things can come together and lead to a real transformation.

My greatest changes came when I discovered who I am in Christ and began to actually believe it. Can you imagine the difference between trying to live out love and marriage in your own power, versus letting the Spirit live in and through you each moment of the day? In one instance, you find yourself trying harder every day only to fail. In the other, you're grabbing a hold of His promises and experiencing the freedom that comes from surrendering to His plan.

If you will get your thinking right in this area of your life, when your husband says something unkind or treats you poorly, your mind will go to what you've practiced. Instead of just biting your tongue, staying silent, and calmly moving onto the next subject, focus on having the right heart. It's much easier to do the things we are called to do when we allow Jesus to be at the forefront of our hearts and minds. When Jesus is behind our actions and decisions, a true and lasting impact can be made.

Our transformation is guaranteed when we are complete in Christ, but God did not save us with the intent that we spend the rest of our lives trying harder to please Him through our own human strength. He wants to be an active participant in our lives, and we make that happen each and every time we choose to walk in His Spirit. We must live out who we have already become in Christ by allowing His goodness, love, and righteousness to manifest themselves through our behavior. The degree to which we believe that Jesus is capable of changing us will be revealed in the way we live each and every moment of the day.

Choose to take Jesus with you on your journey to godliness and you'll find that a sanctified marriage will be the result. When I began to put Jesus first, everything He asked me to do became much easier. The more times you do the right thing, the more your mind will develop the patterns necessary to make godliness with contentment second nature.

Am I perfect? In Christ, yes, but in practice I have a ways to go. Am I godly and righteous? In Christ, yes, because He calls me holy and gives me His righteousness. Am I God's beloved child? I must be because He promised it, even in the times that I fail.

If you stumble and fall, pick yourself back up by remembering who God says you are, and then go forward to make it right. It has taken me years to learn the difference between an argument and a discussion; between a joke and a snide remark; and between truly not feeling well and just using illness as an excuse not to do what God asks of me in my marriage. It's much easier to know the difference between these things when I allow God's Spirit to convict, exhort, and encourage me.

In closing, thank you for choosing to walk beside me as I glanced back on my journey to transformation. My hope and prayer is that you'll find the same joy and peace I have in believing all of God's Word and walking in His ways. Learn from Jesus and an older godly woman; be completely open to wherever He wants to take you. I've had the good, the bad, and the ugly in my life, and I wouldn't change a thing because of where I am now. Yes, I could have done with a lot less pain, but look at what I have been blessed with: four beautiful children who are all happily married to godly spouses, a generation of godly grandchildren being raised up by parents who love the Lord, and a good husband who shares life with me at the deepest level possible. We walk, we talk, we laugh, and we cry together. We both want to first please God and then each other out of an imperfect love and complete commitment.

I am transformed by God, completely brand new in Christ, washed by the blood of Jesus, filled with His Spirit, and a child of the King. You can be the same way too. Now let's go live it out!

SOME FINAL THOUGHTS FROM KEN

Lastly, I want to share a few closing thoughts from my husband, Ken, who witnessed my transformation firsthand:

> It's sometimes hard to remember the past struggles in our marriage when things are so good now. God has taken our hard times and transformed them into an amazing marriage, wonderful children, and a whole family that is set on pleasing the Lord.
>
> I won't rehash the past, as both Lori and I made mistakes we wish we could take back. My greatest sin against Lori over the years was my unkind responses to her remarks of dissatisfaction about me. I wish I had just been taught, as I now teach other husbands, to stop jumping in the mud with your spouse when they disrespect you or are difficult to deal with. Oh, to have been Jesus to my wife day by day, moment by moment, instead of showing her the same unkindness she showed me. Why does it take years to learn the simple idea that two wrongs never make a right, and that punishing your wife with words will never get her to change?
>
> Somewhere around our twentieth year of marriage, I decided I wanted to practice all the disciplines of the Christian life. I began to systematically cross them off a list and, in doing so, saw the need to clean up my reactions to Lori. Years of arguing and being told I needed to do things her way had taken such a toll on me that even her smallest requests or pithy comments could set off my frustrations with her.

Lori: "Do you want a salad tonight?"

Me: "There you go again, trying to feed me rabbit food . . ."

Lori: "I was just asking if you want a salad or not."

It's ironic that for the past ten years or so I have mainly eaten huge salads with roasted chicken on top five to six nights a week. I get plenty of comfort-food dinners when I'm out on the road, so I love the crisp, clean salads that Lori makes for me each night. The problem, however, was never with the salad itself, but with her desire to control so many areas of my life.

What I really craved more than anything back then was to be able to have a true connection with my wife: to be at peace with her and not have so many conversations that turned into arguments, to have her love and accept me just the way I am, and to know she fully understood my deepest fears, desires, and secrets. I couldn't share those things with her back then out of fear that she would have even more areas to find fault with me.

There's no greater sense of relief and peace than knowing that no matter what I do or say, my Transformed Wife will be at peace. Lori may not like it, and she may even say something about it, but she will deal with me in a graceful, loving, and respectful manner, honoring me as the one God gave to be her husband.

Such love and acceptance carries with it a great responsibility for the husband who is set on pleasing His Lord and Savior. If a disobedient husband can be won by his wife's godly behavior, how much more is the godly husband moved to give love, affection, and kindness to a submissive and respectful wife?

I love the way Lori changed her arguing habit. I remember when she was reading *Created to Be His Help Meet* and we had this conversation. "Ken, I finally figured it out," she said.

"What's that?" I inquired.

"How we can have an intimate marriage."

I liked hearing that, but there had to be a catch. "Okay, what do I need to do now?

"It's nothing you need to do," she said as she looked sheepishly to the ground. "What has to happen is that I need to please you."

"I like the way that sounds!" I exclaimed as I started up the stairs to my office. The next thing I knew, she was right behind me as I sat down at my desk. "What can I do right *now* to please you?" she asked.

I was shocked and surprised to hear her say that. In our home, I basically took care of myself in almost every aspect, except for the laundry and house cleaning. Lori took care of the kids and made them healthy foods, and I took care of myself and made my own entrées or meals, which the kids often ate with me after having their salads. I did my own shopping for food and for clothes, and I did my own ironing. I had been trained to take care of myself and help out with the kids, especially since I lived with a very sick wife for much of our marriage. Since this was the case in our marriage, you can see why I was so dumbfounded by Lori's question regarding how she could please me.

"Well, you know . . . my ironing isn't done, so maybe

you could iron some shirts for me," I said. "That way I won't have to scramble to get that done before I hop on the next plane."

Lori ran off to iron my shirts. Ten minutes later, she returned to my office and said, "You know, ironing is really hard with my bad neck. Could I maybe do two to three shirts a day? By the end of the week, I should have all of your shirts ironed."

Who wouldn't appreciate that can-do attitude? I looked at her and said, "Lori, I'm just happy you even *want* to please me."

Her face turned a shade of red. "You don't believe me, do you?"

"Lori, it's not that I don't believe you want to please me. It's just that all we ever seem to do is argue. If I say it's gray, you say it's black. If I say it's round, you say it's oval. We hardly agree on anything."

It was then that the most remarkable thing happened. I can't explain it completely and it took me a week or so to really believe it, but when Lori stuck out her hand to shake mine, she spoke the most beautiful words my ears had ever heard in our marriage: "We will never argue again."

Full of conviction, Lori made an impossible promise to keep. Yet I knew what those words really meant: Lori was not saying that she would *never* argue with me again, but that we would finally live in peace and harmony together.

I smiled. "Can I test you?"

"Sure."

For the next few days, I put her to the test, but she never took the bait. Then one evening, with two teenagers on each side of the dinner table as witnesses, Lori and I were flirting with each other and laughing just like we did in the old days before we were married. That's when it hit me: I was more madly in love with this woman than ever before.

The discord, stress, fighting, and disconnect was gone. Her frowns had turned to smiles every time I walked into the room. Her dissatisfaction with my choices was met with a gentle question, "Are you sure? Let me know if I can help you with it."

The angst in my heart was healing, and I was beginning to feel like someone who was finally comfortable in my own skin under my own roof. I was home at last, and my wife, who was suffering with a yet-to-be-discovered brain tumor, had vulnerably chosen to do things God's way because she loved Him and loved me.

We both had lots to work on, but we've had fun doing it together. Instead of defending our rights, we invited each other to call out sin wherever we saw it in our home, but we did this in such a way that it fit with God's design of me as the respected leader and Lori as my cheerful and submissive follower.

Love casts out fear, and knowing that all we have to do is rest in Him who lives through us gives the both of us the confidence to keep pressing forward every day. God has transformed us by His great and mighty salvation, not only for heaven, but even in the here and now. We invite you to join us in a life of sanctification, becoming who you already are in Christ Jesus, the one we call

Lord. Choose to do as He says so you may enter into all of God's promises for this life and the next.

The apostle Peter tells us clearly who you are once Jesus has come to make His home in your life:

> *But you are a chosen race, a royal priesthood, a holy nation, a people for God's own possession, so that you may proclaim the excellencies of Him who has called you out of darkness into his marvelous light.*
>
> 1 Peter 2:9 (NASB).

> *Grace and peace be multiplied to you in the knowledge of God and of Jesus our Lord. seeing that His divine power has granted to us everything pertaining to life and godliness, through the true knowledge of Him who called us by His own glory and excellence. For by these He has granted to His precious and magnificent promises, having escaped the corruption that is in the world by lust.*
>
> 2 Peter 1:2-4 (NASB)

Study these verses just for a moment and look at the many promises contained therein. It's in knowing who you are in Christ that allows God's transforming power to radically change your marriage into one flesh. You choose an abundant and free life in Christ Jesus when you leave behind your own stubborn will and exchange it for His will and ways.

What Lori has shared so far is our story, and we are sticking with it to the end. By the grace of

God, we're no longer two individuals tossed to and fro by reacting to unkind words or selfishness. Instead, we hold on tightly to the promises of God. We are not of this world but of the Kingdom of God that exists everywhere in the hearts and minds of all who love Him and are called according to His purposes. His greatest promise for marriage is that "the two shall become one." One mind, one heart, one purpose, and one common love for Jesus.

We are to have a most reasonable faith. If at any time you're told by others—or even us—about something you find to be unreasonable, go to the Word of God and check it out. We don't want you to take our advice for anything other than pointing you back to His Word. When I see Lori studying her Bible diligently, seeking to share the Good News with others, and putting off the things she once considered "needs" that now are mere desires, I see a beautiful and godly woman whom I enjoy growing old with.

Let me finish with a story. On the morning of our wedding, I was inspired to write something for my bride. Little did I know how prophetic these words would become in our marriage. They are words I held onto tightly when I felt all hope was lost to ever see my beautiful bride happy and content with me in marriage. These lines of poetry anchored me and kept me focused on the task of remaining true to my vows, true to my bride, and, most of all, true to my Lord Jesus:

A Struggler's Promise

Take my hand, I'll lead you on,
through joy and sorrow, love's endeavor;
I'm by your side, the victory's won,
your life is mine forever.

A wedding bell's no easy song,
the commitment of life to each other;
To seek for you the best, no wrong,
this is to love your brother.

To join our lives and become one,
a life of love each day;
A struggler's promise, "til life is done,"
working together to find the way.

We want to live our lives together,
to struggle and laugh and cry,
We'll sail the seas of stormy weather,
fight for love, willing to die.

Why should two become one,
if love holds trials and fear?
If hearts and minds become stunned,
by the person we hold so dear?

The answer lies in love you see,
struggles will help us grow;
For only through pain it seems can be,
the commitment of love that two can know.

For God is using you for me,
to help me become love;
I'll grow like Christ, in Him I'll be,
kind and considerate of you my love.

We can't forget love's purpose here,
for Christ is the one we wed,
He's the one who holds us dear,
my Lord's the one who said:

"Take my hand I'll lead you on,
through joy and sorrow, love's endeavor;
I'm by your side, the victory's won,
your lives are mine . . . together."

Ken Alexander, December 1980

About the Author

LORI ALEXANDER, author of *The Power of a Transformed Wife*, is a wife, mother, grandmother, homemaker, writer, mentor to young women, and a follower of Jesus Christ.

Lori grew up thirty miles north of downtown Los Angeles in Canyon Country, California, as the oldest of three daughters to Art and Ellen. She attended Westmont College, a Christian institute of higher learning, in Santa Barbara, where she met Ken Alexander. After graduating with a degree in liberal arts and earning her teaching credential, she and Ken married and settled near her hometown, where she became a first-grade school teacher.

Following the birth of her second child, Lori realized how much their children needed her at home full time. With Ken's blessing, she made the decision to come home for good and went on to eventually raise their four wonderful children. Now married for thirty-five years, she and Ken have been blessed with five grandchildren so far.

With her love of mentoring, Lori started blogging in 2011, teaching women how to love their husbands and children, as well as be keepers of their home. Her posts—seen as controversial by some and a common-sense return to biblical values by others—started being shared by thousands, then tens of thousands, and now millions. To date, more than 5 million have visited her website and been impacted by her teachings. Lori is dedicated to continue teaching truth to women for as long as the Lord allows, and she hopes to reach many millions more in the years to come.

Visit Lori Alexander online at www.lorialexander.blogspot.com.

Made in the USA
Columbia, SC
18 April 2022

59120326R00133